Poetry Ireland Review 98

Eagarthóir/Editor

Caitríona O'Reilly

Poetry Ireland Ltd/Éigse Éireann Teo gratefully acknowledges the assistance of The Arts Council/An Chomhairle Ealaíon and The Arts Council of Northern Ireland.

Poetry Ireland invites individuals and commercial organisations to become Friends of Poetry Ireland. For more details please contact:

Poetry Ireland Friends Scheme
Poetry Ireland
2 Proud's Lane
off St Stephen's Green
Dublin 2
Ireland

or telephone +353 1 4789974; e-mail management@poetryireland.ie

PATRONS:
Joan and Joe McBreen ColourBooks Ltd

Poetry Ireland Review is published quarterly by Poetry Ireland Ltd. The Editor enjoys complete autonomy in the choice of material published. The contents of this publication should not be taken to reflect either the views or the policy of the publishers.

ISBN: 1-902121-36-8
ISSN: 0332-2998

ASSISTANT EDITOR: Paul Lenehan, with the assistance of Lucile Dumont, Laura Jacobs, Conor Leahy and Jessica Colley

DESIGN: Alastair Keady (**www.hexhibit.com**)
Printed in Ireland by **ColourBooks Ltd** Baldoyle Industrial Estate Dublin 13

Contents — Poetry Ireland Review 98

Seamus Heaney

'HAD I NOT BEEN AWAKE…'

Had I not been awake I would have missed it,
A wind that rose and whirled until the roof
Pattered with quick leaves off the sycamore

And got me up, the whole of me a-patter,
Alive and ticking like an electric fence;
Had I not been awake I would have missed it

It came and went so unexpectedly
And almost it seemed dangerously,
Returning like an animal to the house,

A courier blast that there and then
Lapsed ordinary. But not ever
Afterwards. And not now.

Seamus Heaney

LAPSE OF TIME

i
Now the oil-fired heating boiler comes to life
Abruptly, drowsily, like the timed collapse
Of a sawn down tree, another time and lapse

That must have fallen around midsummer
Come swimming up, and the place, it dawns on me,
Could have been Grove Hill before the trees were cut,

Where I often stood with them on airy Sundays
Shin-deep in hilltop bluebells, looking out
At Magherafelt's four spires in the distance.

Too late, alas, now for the apt quotation
About a love that's proved by steady gazing
Not at each other but in the same direction.

ii
Quercus, the oak. And *Quaerite*, seek ye.
Among green leaves and acorns in mosaic
(Our college arms surmounted by *columba*,

Dove of the church, of Derry's sainted grove)
The footworn motto stayed indelible:
Seek ye first the Kingdom... Fair and square

I stood on in the Junior House hallway
There is a grey eye will look back
Seeing them as a couple, I now see,

For the first time, all the more together
For having had to turn and walk away, as close
In the leaving (or closer) as in the getting.

iii
It's winter at the seaside where they've gone
For the wedding meal. And I am at the table,
Uninvited, ineluctable.

A skirl of gulls. A smell of cooking fish.
Plump dormant silver. Stranded silence. Tears.
Their bibbed waitress unlids a clinking dish

And leaves them to it, under chandeliers.
And to all the anniversaries of this
They are not ever going to observe

Or mention even in the years to come.
And now the man who drove them here will drive
Them back, and by evening we'll be home.

iv
Were I to have embraced him anywhere
It would have been on the riverbank
That summer before college, him in his prime,

Me at the time not thinking how he must
Keep coming with me because I'd soon be leaving.
That should have been the first, but it didn't happen.

The second did, at New Ferry one night
When he was very drunk and needed help
To do up his trouser buttons. And the third

Was on the landing during his last week,
Helping him to the bathroom, my right arm
Taking the webby weight of his underarm.

v
It took a grandson to do it properly,
To rush in and surprise him in the armchair
With a snatch raid on his neck,

Proving him thus vulnerable to delight,
Coming as great proofs often come
Of a sudden, one off, then the steady dawning

Of whatever *erat demonstrandum*.
Just as a moment back a son's three tries
At an embrace in Elysium

Swam up into my very arms, and in and out
Of the Latin stem itself, the phantom
Verus that has slipped from 'very'.

Peter Sirr

'IN STEP WITH WHAT ESCAPED ME': THE POETRY OF SEAMUS HEANEY

> This is the introductory essay included with *Seamus Heaney: Collected Poems*, a 15-CD box set of Seamus Heaney reading his eleven poetry collections, published by RTÉ/The Lannan Foundation.

Two years ago I was driving along a country road near Strokestown in Co Roscommon. It was dark and I was slightly nervous because I didn't know the road well and I was looking for the local secondary school in whose assembly hall Seamus Heaney would be giving a reading. Suddenly out of the darkness loomed a huge ash tree on whose branches I could make out a large cardboard sign with the words 'Seamus Heaney' in luminous paint and an arrow pointing to a lane on the right. The improvised sign, the reading that followed to a packed and enthralled audience, and the excitement afterwards, testified to a popularity and a rapport with readership and audience very unusual even in a country which grants occasional notice to poets and poetry. John Banville caught this aspect well in the foreword he wrote to the edition of Seamus Heaney that *The Guardian* issued in its *Great Poets of the 20th Century* series in 2008. 'Few poets find a way into the inner ear of the multitude,' he said. Banville's point was also that it's unusual for a poetry of this order to insinuate itself into the public affection, a poetry that offers complex witness to the physical and psychical disturbances of violence at the same time as lyric celebration of the familiar, poems that can be, as the poet himself has put it, 'odd as odd and hard and contrary'.

The poems *The Guardian* chose to publish that St Patrick's Day reinforce that point: 'The Tollund Man', for instance, – an iconic, emblematic Heaney poem from *Wintering Out* which connects an Iron Age sacrificial victim with a lost, unhappy contemporary reality and does this with a language that is chiselled, deliberate and strange even as it implicates us in its intimacy. Or a poem like 'The Toome Road', which marks out the poet's territory as it registers the intrusion of armoured cars 'camouflaged with broken alder branches' – there are whole worlds in that poem, real, spiritual, mythological, a kind of material possession of habitat and human imprint and potential rupture, reminding us that this is how Heaney works, by operating across several layers, by inhabiting the different domains of the possible, by reconfiguring the familiar, as in the title poem of the recent *District and Circle* where a journey in the London Underground is as much a journey into the poet's own past, as much an exploration of the district as of the wider circle.

The strap-hanging figure in the underground train, 'well girded, yet on edge, / Spot-rooted, buoyed, aloof, / Listening to the dwindling noises off' is the poet performing his delicate balancing act on the 'flicker-lit' threshold of past and present, life and death.

So it shouldn't surprise us that his recent work sees the poet testing the old sources again and subjecting them to the pressure of experience and craft. From the outset Seamus Heaney was a poet of extraordinary materiality: the visible world swarmed in to be reconstituted in dense stacks of language – those processions of thickly textured nouns and adjectives, that lust for exactitude, for a language that answered the demands of memory and clanged with the force of hammer on anvil. *District and Circle* is full of the physicality and richly textured responsiveness that announced itself forcefully in *Death of a Naturalist*, the poet's first volume, published in 1966 by Faber and Faber.

What is it about this poetry that appeals to so many and that has, from the outset, earned itself critical acceptance and admiration of a kind rarely seen, establishing a consensus perhaps best summarised by Christopher Ricks when he called Heaney 'the most trusted poet of our islands'? Part of the appeal, certainly, lies in the subject matter. Heaney's consistent imaginative attention to his rural Co Derry upbringing affords many readers the sense, perhaps, that the life he expresses is part of a collective life of the spirit, the life of an Ireland that belongs to our sense of the past. The verbal gifts that he brings to bear on his subjects give the work a sensual presence and an appeal to what Eliot called 'the auditory imagination' that is hard to resist, in the way that Wordsworth, Hardy or Ted Hughes are hard to resist. There is the rich variety of the work: the poems of nature, the love poems, the poetry of memory, the translations, the essays. And yet, from the very beginning, a current of unease runs through the work, a sense that poetry, for all its aesthetic compensations, may not be enough, that the poet is poised, uncomfortably, between 'politics and transcendence', between realism and celebration or between 'the atrocious' and the counterlife of imaginative faith.

Heaney famously signed his early poems 'Incertus', the uncertain one, as if he didn't quite believe his own gift, but an uncertainty principle is built into the work from the start, a kind of duality between affirmation and doubt, imaginative freedom and constraint, that in itself becomes part of the drama of the poetry. The poetry conducts a constant dialogue with itself, weighing itself in the balance, subjecting itself to forensic analysis. The narrative of Heaney's poetic career runs parallel to the political disintegration of Northern Ireland and the ensuing violence, and the uncertainty principle is closely linked to the poet's struggle to come to terms both with the violence itself and the poet's response to it. Heaney has had to bear the weight of public expectation – an expectation as ill-defined as it was pervasive – that poetry should somehow answer to violence, division, rupture, that the poet speaks out of the public domain, that his voice must somehow be representative.

Heaney was not alone in this, of course. His was an extraordinarily gifted generation of poets, and his Northern contemporaries included Derek Mahon and Michael Longley, while following close behind came Paul Muldoon, Medbh McGuckian, Ciaran Carson, all of whom developed their own strategies for writing out of a divided society. Fruitful contradictions are at the heart of Seamus Heaney's work in other ways. To understand Heaney it is necessary to appreciate the complexity of his situation – on the one hand the background as a rural, Catholic nationalist, on the other a powerfully intense relationship with the English language and its poetry tradition. The complications and tensions come gradually into focus. The early work offers a first flourish of the gift, a laying down of the world of childhood in dense, heavy textures. The first thing you notice is the intense physicality and natural finesse of the language:

> All year the flax-dam festered in the heart
> Of the townland;
>
> [...]
>
> Bubbles gargled delicately, bluebottles
> Wove a strong gauze of sound around the smell.
>
> – 'DEATH OF A NATURALIST'

That's what poems like 'Blackberry-Picking', 'Death of a Naturalist', 'Churning Day', 'The Early Purges' do – they weave a strong gauze of sound as they recreate the sensations and rhythms of a farm childhood, as they look for a language that matches the bountiful and yet threatening natural world, that sets it down with a kind of absolute finality. The vision of nature is both realist and numinous – the sense of energies about to break through, or the sense of an alternative configuration of energy, a world near yet remote.

If they often have a monumental quality or the quality of still lifes where the objects seem to clamour themselves on the canvas, the scenes these early poems present are full of foreboding. The dominant images are of rotting, over-ripeness, slime, 'rat-grey fungus'. The early world that is recovered is presented in terms of high drama and subdued violence. The poems are also concerned with art and its making, the articulation of his own search for a distinctive voice. The very first poem is 'Digging', a self-conscious account of the vocation of art and a realisation of how that calling will separate him from the world that the poems evoke:

Between my finger and my thumb
The squat pen rests.
I'll dig with it.

The lines seem canonical now, but 'Digging' was a kind of initiation for Heaney; written in the summer of 1964 it was, he has said, 'the first poem I wrote where I thought my feelings had got into words...' and 'the first place where I felt I had done more than make an arrangement of words: I felt that I had let down a shaft into real life.'[1] It's a prophetic poem in that 'digging', in the sense of excavating, unpeeling layers of the past, is at the core of the work.

Looking back at *Death of a Naturalist*, what strikes one is the confidence of the poems – the confidence of a writer possessing his material. The sense of a writer setting out his stall, testing and trusting his own voice is most clearly articulated in the closing poem of the book, 'Personal Helicon', where the poet evokes the wells of his childhood and converts them into a metaphor for the act of poetry: 'I rhyme / To see myself, to set the darkness echoing.' The book is remarkable for the extent to which early memory shapes and defines it. Throughout his work memory is a trigger and a release into a sense of doubleness, of the intersection of the ordinary and the mysterious which comes through strongly in a poem like 'The Diviner', where, as in 'The Forge' in *Door into the Dark*, an unnamed custodian of a profession that seems to border the real and the imaginary, goes about his business until:

The rod jerked with precise convulsions,
Spring water suddenly broadcasting
Through a green hazel its secret stations.

Door into the Dark is still rooted in memory of the childhood world, and is full of the same intense physicality and observational precision. But if that world is seen for itself it also begins, in poems like 'The Forge', to ramify into symbol or allegory; the rich physical presence of ordinary objects acquire a spiritual density:

All I know is a door into the dark.
Outside, old axles and iron hoops rusting;
Inside, the hammered anvil's short-pitched ring,
The unpredictable fantail of sparks
Or hiss when a new shoe toughens in water.

There's a rhetorical reach in that opening line that echoes the declaration at the end of 'Personal Helicon'. Yet here it's a confession of ignorance, of being outside the mystery which is celebrated by the priest-like figure inside. The blacksmith at work in the darkness is a figure as imagined as real – the poet is on the outside, hesitant and speculative, hovering on the threshold.

Heaney has said that in his earliest poems he tended to turn away from the immediate tensions – sectarianism, underlying violence – of Northern Ireland in favour of the impulse to write a more personal kind of poem, with Ted Hughes as a strong influence: 'one part of my temperament took over: the private Co Derry childhood part of myself rather than the slightly aggravated young Catholic male part.'[2] Yet one of the most striking poems in *Door into the Dark*, 'Requiem for the Croppies', is an explicit identification with his nationalist heritage. Written to commemorate the fiftieth anniversary of the Easter Rising, it returns instead to the 1798 rebellion, and presents an image of continuity and resurrection through the voice of a dead 'croppy':

> The pockets of our greatcoats full of barley –
> No kitchens on the run, no striking camp –
> We moved quick and sudden in our own country.

The worsening political situation in the North meant that such explicit gestures became problematic and for nearly thirty years he didn't read it. If he has sometimes tended to read a reluctance to deal explicitly with the contemporary political situation as a suppression of part of his temperament, we need to remind ourselves that poetry doesn't easily accommodate the kind of commentary sometimes expected of it, but we also need to pay due attention to the nature of his imagination. 'Requiem for the Croppies' is a powerful poem not simply because the poet is writing out his nationalist heritage but because he creates an unforgettable image of endurance out of the 'greatcoats full of barley':

> Terraced thousands died, shaking scythes at cannon.
> The hillside blushed, soaked in our broken wave.
> They buried us without shroud or coffin
> And in August the barley grew up out of the grave.

Heaney's world is now so familiar to his readers that it's important to understand the degree to which his poems map experiences that were not readily available in Irish literature. He has talked of how, for instance, the poetry of Louis MacNeice still felt distant to him, made him feel that he was still 'up against the windowpane of literature'.[3] The world of poetry and literature seemed remote from 'the world of state scholarships, the Gaelic Athletic Association, October devotions, the Clancy Brothers, buckets and egg-boxes where I had had my being.'[4] This is why Patrick

Kavanagh was such a vital figure – he gave Heaney permission to trust his own experience, to make poems, as had Kavanagh, out of 'the unregarded data of the life I had lived', and 'to dwell without cultural anxiety among the usual landmarks of your life.'[5] But much as Heaney's work has valued the specific data of his own background, he has always sought to go beyond the immediately available. *Death of a Naturalist* ended with an artistic statement that saw the poet firmly planted in his own territory, but the inspirational spring was also a prompt 'To see myself, to set the darkness echoing.' *Door into the Dark* again ends with the poet defining his imaginative ground, this time in opposition to another foundation myth, the landscape of American settlement: if 'We have no prairies / To slice a big sun at evening' there is the compelling territory of bogland, one of the heartlands of rural experience, soft, yielding, mysterious and preservative – always ready to offer up iconic emblems of the past:

> They've taken the skeleton
> Of the Great Irish Elk
> Out of the peat, set it up,
> An astounding crate full of air.

By the time that his next book, *Wintering Out*, was published in 1972, Heaney's life had begun to change. He left Queen's University for a sabbatical year in Berkeley, California and, not long after he returned, he moved with his family to Wicklow and then Dublin. The books from this period – *Wintering Out*, *North* (1975) and *Field Work* (1979) are crucial. A deepening sense of the poet's vocation is accompanied by the opening out of the poems' perspectives with their forays into history and myth, and also by a more charged sense of the poet's role and responsibilities. This deepening and the troubled sense of the responsibilities of art in a time of violence were also characteristic of Heaney's contemporaries:

> Somewhere beyond
> The scorched gable end
> And the burnt-out
> Buses there is a poet indulging his
> Wretched rage for order –
>
> Or not as the case
> May be, for his
> Is a dying art,
> An eddy of semantic scruple
> In an unstructurable sea.

– DEREK MAHON, 'RAGE FOR ORDER'

Initially *Wintering Out* seems to be a continuation of the conversation begun by the earlier books. The poems are prompted by archaeology, philology, the lore and lure of place names on their borders of language: Anahorish, Broagh, Toome, Moyola. A new formal pressure is also evident: tense quatrains, a sort of stubby enjambment, thickness of texture, a slowing down, syntactic complexity:

He is wintering out
the back-end of a bad year,
swinging a hurricane-lamp
through some outhouse;

a jobber among shadows.
Old work-whore, slave-
blood, who stepped fair-hills
under each bidder's eye...
–'SERVANT BOY'

The servant boy is a figure, maybe, for a colonial dispossession – landless, little regarded, a hireling 'resentful / and impenitent', and a sign that these poems are actively interested in a cultural recovery, in claiming a 'hoard'. The poems that explore his home territory relish the music and original meaning of place names as well as registering the substratum of the older language: the 'anach fhíor uisce' that lies beneath Anahorish or the 'tawny guttural water' of Moyola.

Landscape, language and history are intimately connected in these poems, and in them we can read the beginning of a certain kind of public poetry, as Heaney seeks ways to represent his own heritage imaginatively and to begin to cope with the fissures of a society now in deep conflict. The prefacing poem, which reappears as part of 'Whatever You Say Say Nothing' in *North*, makes clear the context in which the work of the book proper is to be read; the poet sees the new internment camp from the road:

and it was déjà-vu, some film made
of Stalag 17, a bad dream with no sound.

Is there a life before death? That's chalked up
on a wall downtown. Competence with pain,
coherent miseries, a bite and a sup,
we hug our little destiny again.
–'FOR DAVID HAMMOND AND MICHAEL LONGLEY'

In fact the book is a long way from the kind of journalistic observation and closeness to event this implies. At its centre is 'The Tollund Man', the first of the Bog People poems initially prompted by Heaney's reading of P V Glob's study of the bodies of Iron Age sacrificial victims preserved in Danish bogs. *The Bog People* had a profound impact on Heaney's imagination. The bog is the enabling image for this imaginative continuity with the past, and its continual leakage into the present. The first part of 'The Tollund Man' is a still life contemplation of the photograph and a sympathetic imagining of the man's death and fantastic preservation. The bog-goddess is seen in typically sexual, eroticised terms, demanding death but also providing a preservative afterlife:

> Bridegroom to the goddess,
>
> She tightened her torc on him
> And opened her fen,
> Those dark juices working
> Him to a saint's kept body...

That 'kept body' is brilliant – kept in the sense of preserved, but also in the sense of a kept man. It is as the poem develops that it begins, uneasily, to encompass a contemporary reality. The 'winter seeds' in the Tollund Man's stomach sow an image of a recent murder, but the connection between the two is held in check by the tentative grammar of the gesture:

> I could risk blasphemy,
> Consecrate the cauldron bog
> Our holy ground and pray
> Him to make germinate
>
> The scattered, ambushed
> Flesh of labourers,
> Stockinged corpses
> Laid out in the farmyards,
>
> Tell-tale skin and teeth
> Flecking the sleepers
> Of four young brothers, trailed
> For miles along the lines.

The poem isn't suggesting that the fate of the four murdered brothers is somehow the same as that of the sacrificial victim who died at Aarhus; nor, I think, does it satisfy itself with the suggestion that violence is stitched into the human fabric and that this blood obsession is what links us to this figure. But Heaney's imagination is to an extraordinary extent nourished by ritual – it finds itself through ladders of ritual, it is always reaching for a kind of sacral framework. The Tollund Man is invoked through a kind of sexual-religious apprehension and his image, though an act of sympathetic imagining, calls up the flesh of the murdered men and causes the poet to realise them. The nuanced grammar continues in the concluding section as his imagination works a connection between the two worlds:

> Something of his sad freedom
> As he rode the tumbril
> Should come to me, driving,
> Saying the names
>
> Tollund, Grauballe, Nebelgard,
> Watching the pointing hands
> Of country people,
> Not knowing their tongue.
>
> Out here in Jutland
> In the old man-killing parishes
> I will feel lost,
> Unhappy and at home.

Should come to me – but not necessarily. This is a risky journey. The poet travels from uncertainty to assertion. Saying the names, he chants himself back in time until, suddenly, *here* is Jutland, the 'man-killing parishes'. Again, the poem is not asking us to make an equivalence between the parishes of twentieth-century Ireland and Iron Age Denmark; it is not an act of translation so much as a record of loss precisely because killing is human and therefore bleakly comprehensible. The risk of the poem is what lifts it from exercise. It's a risk that all the Bog People poems take.

North pushes the discoveries of *Wintering Out* to the next stage. It is a more consciously northern book, more explicitly myth-making, and the template established by 'The Tollund Man' is re-used with conscious deliberation. 'Punishment' pushes the risk further, allowing a closer identification of poet and victim. The poet with his conscience, the 'artful voyeur', is as much the subject as the historical victim or her contemporary counterparts in his realisation that he would have cast 'the stones of silence':

> I who have stood dumb
> when your betraying sisters,

cauled in tar,
wept by the railings,

who would connive
in civilised outrage
yet understand the exact
and tribal, intimate revenge.

This is a portrait of the artist as disengaged but comprehending, a combination of intimacy and distance replicated in poems like 'Funeral Rites', 'The Grauballe Man', 'Kinship'. The distance comes from formal deliberation, the meshing of the historical and contemporary perspective, all creating an intimate kind of strangeness that was artistically necessary to Heaney.

There is another kind of detachment in these poems, connecting with their careful, ritualising gesture. The poems are highly conscious of the violent present but they are at pains to detach the poet from any kind of immediate response or partisanship or solution-offering. When he faces The Troubles more directly, in poems like 'Whatever You Say Say Nothing' or 'Singing School' the response is filtered through a self-conscious literary imagination mixed with 'The famous / Northern reticence'. The actual events and their reporting by the media seem to belong to another reality. The conflict is so internalised by those who live there, so buried in circumlocution and strategic banality that any articulation of it, in journalism and poetry, strikes oddly. The poet sits self-consciously in the midst of this, testing his own reactions. The self-questioning reaches its climax in 'Exposure', where the poet, removed from the scene of the Northern conflict in rural Wicklow and waiting for a comet to appear that is part figure for some kind of liberating post-historical revelation, imagines a very different kind of fate, the poet as partisan, committed and engaged , 'a hero / On some muddy compound, / His gift like a slingstone / Whirled for the desperate.'

How did I end up like this?
I often think of my friends'
Beautiful prismatic counselling
And the anvil brains of some who hate me

As I sit weighing and weighing
My responsible *tristia*.
For what? For the ear? For the people?
For what is said behind-backs?

The poem might seem critical of the lack of a direct, absolute, pinnable-down position where the poet is 'neither internee nor informer' but an 'inner émigré, grown long-haired / And thoughtful; a wood-kerne // Escaped from the massacre', but it doesn't posit a viable alternative. It is more an argument for a necessary artistic disengagement than an anxious apologia, and the poem's ambiguous closing image suggests something else, a greater reality, a more powerful and demanding domain which may have been forsaken: 'The once-in-a-lifetime portent, / The comet's pulsing rose.'

Heaney returned to this poem in his Nobel acceptance speech, 'Crediting Poetry', remembering the background of 'listening to the rain in the trees and to the news of bombings closer to home – not only those by the Provisional IRA in Belfast but equally atrocious assaults in Dublin by loyalist paramilitaries from the north.' What he was longing for, he continues, 'was not quite stability but an active escape from the quicksand of relativism, a way of crediting poetry without anxiety or apology.'

Whatever the self-doubting hesitancies of *North*, the poetry that became *Field Work* (1979) shows a renewed confidence and sure-footedness, and a buoyant belief in the power of poetry. Written mainly in rural Wicklow where the poet had moved with his family in 1972 to work full-time as a poet and free-lance writer, the poems happily occupy a more intimate and reflective space than *North* or *Wintering Out*. They are poems of an artistic stocktaking that also engage with the new location. They allow marriage, love, the domestic life to take centre stage, and the volume contains some of Heaney's finest love poems. The book can be read as a declaration of faith in art, and part of its strategy is putting a certain distance between the poet and the domain of public expectation.

Its opening poem, 'Oysters', offers a possible exit from the impasse suggested by 'Exposure'. It presents a scene of worldly sophistication, the self-aware poet enjoying seafood in a restaurant, 'Laying down a perfect memory / In the cool of thatch and crockery.' The language is rich and confident, as if to announce that this will be a book of conscious and confident achievement:

> Our shells clacked on the plates.
> My tongue was a filling estuary,
> My palate hung with starlight:
> As I tasted the salty Pleiades
> Orion dipped his foot into the water.

The poem's – and the book's – internal argument is between pleasure and responsibility, or between freedom and constraint. The anger that doesn't trust the 'Glut of privilege' pushes the poet into 'verb, pure verb'

– a domain of active achievement, maybe, unencumbered by external expectation. The pleasure enacted in language always exists in the shadow of a threat, but the poem can none-the-less be read as a statement of intent. And the poems do have a hard-edged flourish to them. They dispense with the mythic resonances of *North*; they are more firmly grounded in the real; and the elegies, for instance, don't seek to go beyond the lives of the mourned. 'After A Killing' offers a defiant reaffirmation of life in the face of murder:

> And today a girl walks in home to us
> Carrying a basket full of new potatoes,
> Three tight green cabbages, and carrots
> With the tops and mould still fresh on them.

'The Toome Road' shows a new directness, a 'pure verb' approach as it registers the intrusion of British armoured cars in the poet's territory – 'How long were they approaching down my roads / As if they owned them?' – but, for all that the poet might situate himself in his own tradition, there is a growing sense of the complication of the relationship between the poet and 'tribal' values, particularly in a poem like 'Casualty', an elegy for Louis O'Neill, a friend of the poet's killed by a bomb as he broke the curfew imposed by the Provisional IRA after Bloody Sunday. The poem celebrates the wayward individualism of the fisherman, 'Sure-footed but too sly, / His deadpan sidling tact, / His fisherman's quick eye / And turned, observant back.' It also registers the communal funeral of the thirteen shot dead by the Paras. Yet the distinctiveness of the fisherman lay in his refusal to be subject to any bonds – 'he would not be held / At home by his own crowd' – and the poet clearly sympathises with his independent spirit. Even if the poem itself doesn't step outside the bond his unanswered question – 'How culpable was he / That last night when he broke / Our tribe's complicity?' – hangs uneasily throughout the book and suggests the limits of the common bond.

The detachment and the artistic self-placement are evident in the book's central section, 'Glanmore Sonnets' where the poet seeks a re-education in 'the hedge-school of Glanmore', where he hopes to catch 'A voice caught back off slug-horn and slow chanter / That might continue, hold, dispel, appease: / Vowels ploughed into other, opened ground, / Each verse returning like the plough turned round', or 'that moment when the bird sings very close / To the music of what happens.' Yet whatever the consolations of pastoral, and even if '*the end of art is peace*', the shadow of conflict is never far away. The psychic disturbances of the era of the bomb and the hunger strikes find an echo in Dante, in the grotesque image from the *Inferno* of Count Ugolino gnawing at Archbishop

Ruggieri who had locked him up with his sons in a tower in Pisa and left them all to starve to death. Heaney's choice of this scene reinforces our sense of it as in some sense echoing contemporary horror, and his insertion of specific Irish references – Ugolino gnaws at the archbishop who'd imprisoned him 'Like a famine victim at a loaf of bread' – has the effect of localising the horror. 'There's an almost sexual intimacy between Ugolino and Archbishop Roger, which seemed cognate with the violence and intimacy of Ulster,' he said in a conversation with Robert Hass.[6] Dante becomes a haunting and enabling presence for Seamus Heaney at this point. The central sequence of *Station Island* (1984) is a kind of mini *Commedia* where the poet, like Dante, encounters the shades of the dead and must go through an ordeal of self-examination.

Heaney's career at this stage seems to vacillate between freedom and constraint. There's a sense of the poet setting aside some of the burdens of expectation in, for instance, *Sweeney Astray* (1983), his version of the medieval Irish poem 'Suibhne Gealt'. His choice of Sweeney comes partly from the fact that the maddened birdman who flees from the battlefield and takes to the trees offers a parallel for his own situation: 'insofar as Sweeney is also a figure of the artist, displaced, guilty, assuaging himself by his utterance, it is possible to read the work as an aspect of the quarrel between free creative imagination and the constraints of religious, political and domestic obligation.'[7] The freedoms won in *Field Work* and in the gleeful reinvention of Sweeney come under the interrogative glare of 'Station Island', which is structured as a visit to the penitential island of Lough Derg with its stations of the cross, black tea and wakefulness. The pilgrimage to the lake is a central locus of the Catholic experience in Ireland, a microcosm of the journey through experience to repentance and spiritual salvation. Lough Derg is also a much visited literary site, which is itself part of Heaney's subject – William Carleton, Patrick Kavanagh, Denis Devlin wrote significant work inspired by it or, in Carleton's case, reacting against it. Of all of them, Heaney's is the least concerned with the religious significance.

The place of pilgrimage is for Heaney a Dantesque purgatory, an opportunity to summon the ghosts of self-interrogation. Appropriately, two writers book-end the pilgrimage, William Carleton and James Joyce. The most compelling voices in the sequence are the ghosts of the victims of sectarian murder. In revisiting the moments of their deaths Heaney is confronting directly and uncomfortably the deaths themselves and his own responses to them. The poems in *Station Island* create a worrisome zone which continually seems to posit an impossible choice between action and art. The poet consistently refuses the pressure to be conscripted into service, and is also acutely aware of the artistic uselessness of the conflict: 'It is eternally distressing as a political problem, but as a stimulant to the imagination it is almost nil.'[8] The scrupulous resistance of partisanship or propaganda can, however, seem inadequate – the poet can seem to be 'speaking not with forked tongue, but with forked silence.'[9] But if *Station Island* is conceived as a kind of final reckoning with the matter of the North, the ghostly voices offer little in the way of resolution. The most searing criticism comes from Colum McCartney, the poet's slain cousin who directly accuses the poet of having aesthetically prettified his death in the earlier elegy, 'The Strand at Lough Beg':

> You confused evasion and artistic tact.
> The Protestant who shot me through the head
> I accuse directly, but indirectly, you
> who now atone perhaps upon this bed
> for the way you whitewashed ugliness and drew
> the lovely blinds of the *Purgatorio*
> and saccharined my death with morning dew.
>
> – 'STATION ISLAND', VIII

There's a certain relief at the poem's conclusion when the spirit of Joyce appears. His role in the poem is to offer a kind of artistic licence, a permission to fly free of the nets of social or political expectation, to 'strike your note'.

Heaney is at his strongest when he works with the kind of freedom his imagined Joyce counsels. We see something of this freedom in the third part of *Station Island*, in the poems voiced for Sweeney, who is himself a figure for the kind of imaginative escape Heaney seeks.

> Take hold of the shaft of the pen.
> Subscribe to the first step taken
> from a justified line
> into the margin.
>
> – 'THE FIRST GLOSS'

The argument with himself is carried over into *The Haw Lantern* in poems preoccupied with judgment and testing. The book introduces a new vein of allegorical writing, poems like 'From the Frontier of Writing', 'Parable Island', 'From the Republic of Conscience', 'From the Canton of Expectation' and 'The Mud Vision'. One of the most original and impressive poems in the volume, 'The Mud Vision' imagines a country much like Ireland which is afforded a once-off vision of release or possibility, something like the 'comet's pulsing rose' in 'Exposure' which flourishes briefly and disappears, leaving in its wake a fierce sense of what might have been and may yet be:

Our one chance to know the incomparable
And dive to a future. What might have been origin
We dissipated in news. The clarified place
Had retrieved neither us nor itself – except
You could say we survived. So say that, and watch us
Who had our chance to be mud-men, convinced and estranged,
Figure in our own eyes for the eyes of the world.

If these poems seem to be moving as far away as possible from the realm of the autobiographical, the emotional heart of that collection is 'Clearances', the sonnet sequence in memory of the poet's mother, poems that are direct, poised and among the poet's most moving. They return to one of the elemental purposes of poetry, to register a life, to try to enter the cleared space where a life has been, and they do it in a language as plain as possible:

So while the parish priest at her bedside
Went hammer and tongs at the prayers for the dying
And some were responding and some crying
I remembered her head bent towards my head,
Her breath in mine, our fluent dipping knives –
Never closer the whole rest of our lives.
– 'CLEARANCES', III

The central struggle in Heaney's work has been 'to make space in [his] reckoning and imagining for the marvellous as well as for the murderous.'[10] We see this struggle again and again. *Seeing Things* (1991) offers a double vision, the things that are seen, witnessed, materially present, including the finiteness of life itself, and seeing things in the sense of the glimpsed, imagined, hoped for. It begins with Book VI of Virgil, the moment where the Sibyl of Cumae tells Aeneas that the journey back from the underworld will be impossible unless he brings Proserpina the golden bough, as if the gift of poetry, of 'seeing things' is the only way to secure a safe passage back. Much of the journey in this book is down into the past, with poems in memory of the poet's father, and the 'imagined perfection' of things: the pitchfork, the settle bed, a leather schoolbag. But above all it is concerned with the clarity that releases the invisible from the visible, as when, in the title poem, he looks at a cathedral carving of John the Baptist:

Lines
Hard and thin and sinuous represent
The flowing river. Down between the lines
Little antic fish are all go. Nothing else.

And yet in that utter visibility
The stone's alive with what's invisible:
Waterweed, stirred sand-grains hurrying off,
The shadowy, unshadowed stream itself.
All afternoon, heat wavered on the steps
And the air we stood up to our eyes in wavered
Like the zig-zag hieroglyph for life itself.

Seeing Things also contains the sequence 'Squarings', a set of forty-eight twelve-line poems in four sections – one of the freest, most adventurous and unpinnable-down of his works. The poems here are happy to remove themselves from the provable, the concrete, and dwell in the realm of the spirit, in 'anglings, aimings, feints and squints' or in one meaning of the word 'lightening': 'A phenomenal instant when the spirit flares / With pure exhilaration before death'. The poems work in a fast, instinctual procession of image and action, a series of 'shifting brilliancies', poem leading to poem by association. The looseness of the form and organisational principle allows Heaney's instinctive gifts of 'perfected vision' to shine through. There is in this later Heaney a conscious movement to 'Omnipresence, equilibrium, brim', an attempt to balance the earnest apprehension of the real and the visible with a kind of artistic floating or walking on air. Heaney's poetry is never simply one or the other; there is a constant dialectic between them. The push to the airy clarity and brilliancies of 'Squarings' depends on the earth-bound mud visions, it's the acknowledgement of the earthbound that prompts the desire for a transcendent exultation.

We see the two sides of the Heaney temperament clearly in *The Spirit Level*, the first collection after the poet received the Nobel Prize in 1995. 'St Kevin and the Blackbird', in which Kevin out of charity or empathetic excess allows the blackbird to roost in his hands and lets the eggs hatch, provides an image both of art – 'since the whole thing's imagined anyhow' – and the self-forgetting artist who wants 'To labour and not seek reward':

A prayer his body makes entirely
For he has forgotten self, forgotten bird
And on the riverbank forgotten the river's name.

On the other hand, the violence and unconsoled force of 'The Mycenae Lookout' suggest how readily the ideal is compromised by the brute force of reality. It tells the story of Agamemnon, Clytemnestra and Cassandra after the Trojan War, and the lookout might be taken as a figure for the poet, given short shrift by Cassandra: 'No such thing / as innocent / bystanding.' The classical myth allows the poet to express some of the anger he felt in the aftermath of the 1994 ceasefire 'at the waste of lives and friendships and possibilities in the years that had preceded it'.[11] It's as if the poem takes the opportunity of the cessation to shine the full glare of his torch on 'That killing-fest, the life-warp and world-wrong' which 'still augured and endured.'

*

In some ways Heaney's is a remarkably consistent work. The reach and ambition might grow from book to book but the poetry is faithful to the territory mapped out from the start, and each collection continues to circle obsessively round the source. Again and again, memory is the trigger that releases the poetry. Heaney is like a still life artist who needs to arrange the loved and familiar world so that it can shine back its power and strangeness. The later books all draw from the well of the past, and often revisit his own previous configurations of it, so that there is a constant dialogue with himself as poet. The poet twice revisits 'The Tollund Man' to measure the distance travelled since the first outing. In 'The Tollund Man in Springtime', in *District and Circle*, the strangely contemporary figure hovering over 'check-out lines, at cash-points, in those queues / Of wired, far-faced smilers' is also a guardian-like figure come to release Heaney from his Parnassian obligations. He has described him as a kind of releasing revenant: 'He came again to remind me that lyric poetry was OK. The Tollund Man releases me into pleasure.'[12] This is a theme of the later work, a sense of release out of obligation into an airier style, and a style, as he put it, less of stained glass than of plain window glass. *The Spirit Level* opens with 'The Rain Stick' and the instrument becomes the perfect image of joyful imagination: 'Who cares if all the music that transpires // Is the fall of grit or dry seeds through a cactus? / You are like a rich man entering heaven / Through the ear of a raindrop. Listen now again.'

The poems in these later books are also sharpened by their awareness of mortality. Part of Heaney's backward glance is a consolidation of faith in the face of obliteration, as in the memorable image in 'Clearances' of the felled chestnut tree which had been planted at his birth, 'Its heft and hush become a bright nowhere, / A soul ramifying and forever / Silent, beyond silence listened for.' A persistent vein of elegy makes itself felt. *Electric Light* and *District and Circle*, in particular, are haunted by death; there are elegies for Czesław Miłosz, Ted Hughes, George Seferis, and the superb 'The Lift' for his sister.

*

One of the difficulties of writing about Seamus Heaney is that inevitably you end up talking a lot about the themes and concerns of the work.

This is fine on some levels; there is, after all, a distinct Heaney set of concerns, a distinct trajectory and narrative where each collection can be slotted, and because the work itself is highly reflexive the different stances and arguments are actually embedded in the poetry, so that you could very easily only discuss the content and subjects. This can make it easy to miss what is truly valuable and unmissable. We don't go to poets for the whole story of their work; we rarely even go to poets for the specifics of what they say. We go because we are led by our ears, our instincts, because of the way a particular configuration of language operates on mind, heart, body and won't let us go. We go because a particular arrangement of lines seems so absolutely true and unimaginable in any other way that we want to look and listen repeatedly.

> There was a sunlit absence.
> The helmeted pump in the yard
> heated its iron,
> water honeyed
>
> in the slung bucket...
> – FROM 'MOSSBAWN', I. 'SUNLIGHT'

I go back to this poem for the power of its images and their emotional weight, but also to admire the tight poise of the lines and how they break, for the verb 'honeyed' and the 'slung bucket'; and for the unforgettable concluding image of love:

> like a tinsmith's scoop
> sunk past its gleam
> in the meal-bin.

Or I go back to a poem like 'Höfn' for its turbo-charged Anglo-Saxon pith:

> The three-tongued glacier has begun to melt.
> What will we do, they ask, when boulder-milt
> Comes wallowing across the delta flats
>
> And the miles-deep shag-ice makes its move?
> I saw it, ridged and rock-set, from above,
> Undead grey-gristed earth-pelt, aeon-scruff...

Or again, I go back to 'Squarings' for the darting intelligence which, you feel, can snag anything, and its sense of life zigzagging like a hare in and out of the known. 'Seventh heaven may be / The whole truth of a sixth sense come to pass':

At any rate, when light breaks over me
The way it did on the road beyond Coleraine
Where wind got saltier, the sky more hurried

And silver lamé shivered on the Bann
Out in mid-channel between the painted poles,
That day I'll be in step with what escaped me.

Everyone will go back to their own poems for their own reasons; there is an astonishing richness of work to choose from. Again and again the poetry of Seamus Heaney discovers the release into pleasure that is one of the truest sources of all poetry, and if we attend to it we might learn, like the poet, to be in step with what escapes us.

[1] Seamus Heaney, 'Feeling into Words' in *Finders Keepers: Selected Prose* 1971-2001 (Faber and Faber, 2002), p. 14

[2] Seamus Heaney, 'Unhappy and at Home', interview by Seamus Deane, *Crane Bag* 1:1 (Spring 1977), p. 63

[3] Seamus Heaney, 'The Placeless Heaven: Another Look at Patrick Kavanagh' in *Finders Keepers: Selected Prose* 1971-2001 (Faber and Faber, 2002), p. 139

[4] *Ibid.*, p. 139

[5] *Ibid.*, p. 140

[6] Seamus Heaney and Robert Hass, 'Sounding Lines: The Art of Translating Poetry' (9 February 1999), Doreen B Townsend Centre for the Humanities, *Occasional Papers*, Paper 20.

[7] Seamus Heaney, *Sweeney Astray* (Faber and Faber, 1983), viii

[8] In an interview with Francis X Clines, *New York Times*, 13 March 1983

[9] *Ibid.*

[10] Seamus Heaney, 'Crediting Poetry', in *Opened Ground: Poems 1966-1996* (Faber and Faber, 1998), p. 458

[11] In an interview with Henri Cole, *The Paris Review* 144, p. 136

[12] In an interview with Sam Leith, *Daily Telegraph*, 6 April 2006

Barra Ó Seaghdha

EAR OF THE BEHEARER

Seamus Heaney, *Collected Poems*, 15-CD box set (RTÉ and The Lannan Foundation, 2009), €74.95.

With its restrained earthen reds, browns and yellows, with its simple photograph and clean typeface, there is something modest and unflashy about the box in which the recorded version of Seamus Heaney's *Collected Poems* comes to us. At the same time, there is something almost grandiose about the project that has resulted in the emergence of this little box. No Irish poet has ever been publicly celebrated as comprehensively as Heaney has this year, with the near-simultaneous arrival of *Stepping Stones* (a substantial review of his life and writing career in interview with Dennis O'Driscoll), a near-takeover of RTÉ Radio One on the big day (Heaney's seventieth), a television portrait by Charlie McCarthy, an RTÉ-sponsored celebration at IMMA, the related commissioning of works by Irish composers, numerous interviews, features and reviews in both print and broadcast media, and of course our little box.

With the importance of TV, radio and recordings of all kinds in our daily lives, it is hardly surprising that the voices of most of the major English-language poets of the last fifty years have been captured. Here in Ireland, starting in the 1960s, Claddagh Records issued single and double LPs of Irish and Scottish writers such as Patrick Kavanagh, John Montague, Derek Mahon, Seamus Heaney, Hugh MacDiarmid and Sorley MacLean. More recently, we have had Heaney's joint venture with the piper Liam O'Flynn and the double CD of Thomas Kinsella reading his own work. Poets who never or rarely read in public are now the exception. Reading is part of the job of creating an audience and of selling books, and there are more and more readers who will want a recording of their favoured poets for home consumption. But in Heaney's case we are now offered, not a taste or a few alluring tapas, not a lunch or a three-course dinner, but the full menu, dish after dish, from top to bottom, and demanding numerous sittings even from the gluttonous.

That there will be gluttons out there goes without saying. Almost any Heaney-connected product is guaranteed success at the moment: the poetry books sell at a rate that would leave many novelists envious; *Stepping Stones* will deservedly earn itself long-term readership; and it's standing room only, even in large venues, for any public reading by Heaney. Our 15-CD box might seem scaled more to the Transcontinental Highway or the Oriental Express, but why shouldn't a literary train-traveller listen to

Heaney between Portarlington and Ballinasloe? And a motorist might do worse than stick *Wintering Out* in the sound system on one of those rare days when the soul seems to demand more than another snip of classical ear-fodder from Snooze FM or Joe Duffy's relentless eking-out of Mrs Durcan's troubles with her neighbour's terrier and Mr Boland's indignant bark back. If a lyric is worth reading, it is worth lingering over. It may indeed demand lingering over. This is where listening and our own silent reading of a poem diverge.

You are reading the third section of 'Viking Dublin: Trial Pieces'. It could go like this: 'Like a long sword / sheathed in its moisting / burial clays...' *Moisting*, not moist? Hmm... 'Like a long sword / sheathed in its moisting / burial clays, / the keel stuck fast// in the slip of the bank, / its clinker-built hull...' Just a second, are we still talking bones here? What was that earlier? Yes: 'the nostril / is a migrant prow / sniffing the Liffey...' Back to 'clinker-built': 'its clinker-built hull' – that has the crunch of the real about it – 'its clinker-built hull' / spined and plosive / as *Dublin*.' Things keep shifting here. What is being compared to what? Must come back to this and work out exactly how that happens. 'And now we reach in / for shards of the vertebrae...' You go on, pausing here and there, rereading a phrase, moving on till you reach the end. Then, perhaps, after savouring or working out some of the detail, you read again for the pleasure of feeling the whole thing unfold. This kind of to-ing and fro-ing, the flicking to a word or a line in another poem, the breaking and re-knotting of threads, is excluded as the poet's voice moves relentlessly on. (Could the gap between tracks have been longer, allowing the listener a little more time to reflect and absorb, to stare at the ceiling, without hitting the pause button?)

As a reader, you can set your own pace. You are working towards your own reading of the poem and there is nobody to interfere. When you listen to Heaney on CD, either you are getting a preliminary reading that gives you some sense of the poem (but which leaves you still needing to make the poem your own) or you are checking Heaney's version against yours.

If there is something excessive about the whole enterprise, the same cannot be said about Heaney's reading style in individual poems. We can only guess how long the recordings took and how much preparation went into them, but the likelihood is that Heaney did not have to agonise too much over stresses and speeds. For someone who can draw superstar crowds, his delivery is almost invariably steady, unfussed and intimate. Heaney is blessed with a voice that is easy on the ear but, as readers of *Stepping Stones* will know, he is as professional and as respectful of his audience in this aspect of his work as in any other. Seeing that reading was to be an important part of his life as a full-time writer, he worked on his enunciation and projection, attaining clarity, continuity and flexibility of line without sacrificing either his accent or the gift of intimacy that seems to be part of his nature. The stress is not on the voice in itself, or on the poet's personality, but on transmitting as much as possible of the meaning and energy of the poem in this single act of communication.

Again, we can only speculate as to what Heaney felt while reading, as he was obliged to do after agreeing to the project, poems which he had not revisited in years, poems that would have no chance of appearing in the definitive *Selected Poems*. While Heaney's voice sometimes takes on a particular animation, there is no throwaway reading, even of such early poems as 'Gravities' or 'Valediction', where the voice of the poem is not Heaney's. Each poem is given a decent start in life and sent out to fare for itself in the world of the listener, or the ear of the behearer, as a Dewey Redman album title puts it. This necessarily egalitarian approach means that we are reminded of poems that, after a number of readings, we tend to skip or almost erase from memory. In the case of *Death of a Naturalist*, I had forgotten entirely the poem 'The Folk Singers', which targets that awful goody-goody, prettily arranged style of folk-singing that probably drove Bob Dylan howling into his jangling, electric phase. Listening to the poem 'Saint Francis and the Birds', I was suddenly carried back to the young Seán Dunne's reading of his own Saint Francis poem, in a semi-chanting style full of vibrato.

There are indeed many different ways of reading a poem, but some are only effective in performance or in limited doses. Would listening for hours to the Yeats chant be bearable? Heavily stressed reading styles can quickly become painful or monotonous and, for those not swayed by a particular poet's charm, can have the effect of drawing attention to banality of language (I ASKed my MOTHer WHY she USED a SOUP SPOON / to STIR the TEA). Several exponents of this style are active on the Irish scene. In contrast with this and other reading styles that demand either full adhesion or termination with extreme prejudice, Heaney's voice can fade to a pleasant background noise if the listener loses concentration. Print addicts who listen book in hand will very quickly stop listening, as the eye speeds ahead of the ear even when a poem is being read perfectly.

To the question, 'Do he do the police in different voices?', the answer in Heaney's case is a qualified no. There is basically one mode of delivery (within which there can be accelerations and changes of pressure), but there is a second voice (with its own minor variations) that can appear when, for example, children or other people, oracles even, speak in a poem, or when a child's view of the world is being evoked. This merely confirms that Heaney is an excellent performer of his own poetry but not a natural actor, not a flitter from persona to persona.

Even when the reader is the author, today's performance of a poem is just one of many valid possibilities. Speed, stress and other interpretative factors may all vary. Thus, the 'Sunlight' section of 'Mossbawn' (the body of the poem, excluding title and sub-title) takes about five seconds longer in the Poetry Archive version than in the box-set. Does this have the effect of further slowing time and lengthening the 'long afternoon'? Such points of interpretation add to the interest of these recordings. In the 1970s, when reading 'Exposure', did Heaney hammer a little harder on 'the ANvil BRAINS of SOME who HATE me' than he now chooses to do? In fact the line is pronounced quite lightly, with heavy stressing and slowing of 'weighing and weighing' in the same sentence. There is a wistful quality to the way in which the poet allows the last words of the poem – 'the comet's pulsing rose' – almost to drift away.

The emphatic delivery of 'scald, scald, scald' in 'Summer Home' (*Wintering Out*, 1972) is echoed in a later volume (*Field Work*, 1979) when oysters are 'ripped and shucked and scattered', each word receiving full value. Heaney doesn't go much further than this in heightening a line. (The rendering of 'Mid-Term Break' shows that he also knows when understatement is both more effective and more humanly appropriate).

Even if poems are open to multiple interpretations, it is interesting to discover Heaney's own (current) interpretation. The concluding line of 'Digging' is a case in point: Heaney says, 'I'll dig [half-pause] with IT', emphasising the implement over the activity. The first line of another famous early poem, 'The Forge', goes, 'All I know is a door into the dark.' Stressing the 'All' suggests the meaning, 'Everything I know...'; stressing 'know' might suggest, 'The only thing I know...'; Heaney stresses the 'All'. Ultimately, however, once a poem is released into the world, it belongs to each one of us as much as to the poet. It is by listening attentively to the poem rather than to the poet's reading of it for us that we decide on our own ideal interpretation. (Is there a parallel here with the idea of the informed conscience?)

In the poem 'Damson', there is relish in Heaney's voice as he evokes the bricks 'tocked and tapped in line'. Perhaps the whole poem is read with such animation but, as a listener who feels that the mythical references in the poem are rather forced, it is difficult to decide whether I am hearing a similarly forced quality in the voice at times or whether I am importing into it my own discomfort with some of the material. A similar difficulty arises with 'The Flight Path'. It is the poems we love that we really want to hear read, but there is always, in theory at least, the possibility of conversion by listening. However, as *The Spirit Level* and *Electric Light* contain little poetry that I love, I am more likely to pluck what I want from those volumes myself than to listen to the poet run through them from beginning to end. Poems like 'Wordsworth's Skates' or 'Planting the Alder' in *District and Circle*, on the other hand, are delivered whole by the poet and may well call out to be heard again.

The box-set – a collaboration between RTÉ and the Lannan Foundation – comes with a hefty booklet that contains, in addition to photographs and a guide to the CDs, a long essay by Peter Sirr. This recapitulates Heaney's career and situates his work in the context of his times; not just a work of analysis, it is also a younger poet's very precisely judged engagement with the marrow of Heaney's work. It will be as useful to readers of the books as to listeners to the CDs.

The books have been launched one by one down the years and have made their way out to sea. Now, a large new vessel is hitting the water. It is too soon to know how it will fare but, as it is already giving pleasure to many, let's wish it well.

Helen Cooney

SENSE-CLEARING

Robert Henryson, translated by Seamus Heaney, *The Testament of Cresseid & Seven Fables* (Faber and Faber, 2009), £12.99.

It is a truth universally acknowledged that Seamus Heaney is fascinated by 'the act of translation': works in translation occupy an unusually large space in the canon of this poet. His awareness of modern 'translation-theory' is evident. He adverts many times to the three principles which Eliot Weinberger – also a poet and translator – identifies as the three motivations for translation, namely: 'advocacy of the work in question'; 'refreshment from a different speech and culture'; and the pleasures of 'writing by proxy'. The fullness of Heaney's understanding of what the act of translation may encompass is expressed in the course of his essay entitled 'Earning a Rhyme', published in *Poetry Ireland Review* 25:

> Literary translation – or version-making or imitation or refraction or whatever one should call the linguistic carry-over that is mediated through a crib – is still an aesthetic activity.

More specifically, in an interview with Dennis O'Driscoll when *Sweeney Astray* was published, Heaney explained that the litmus test for his undertaking the translation of an individual work is his perception of whether 'there's something here for me'. As he approached the eighth-century, Old English epic poem *Beowulf* (until now, his most recent translated text), the Irish, nationalist Heaney must have felt the hieratic, declamatory voice of the 'scop' to be alien to him in all sorts of ways. However, with his characteristic 'wholeness of vision', Heaney for a start recognised a significant resemblance between the shape of the Old English alliterative half-lines and the shape of many of his earliest poems (albeit mediated through the work of Gerard Manley Hopkins and others). Eventually, and having 'raided' the Old English 'word-hoard' and even added some newly-minted kennings, as well as the odd picturesque dialect-word from his native Ulster, Heaney produced (to quote Bernard O'Donoghue's *Irish Times* review of *Beowulf*), 'a miraculous mix of the poem's original spirit and [his own] voice'. Against all the odds, Heaney gradually found common ground with the earliest poem in the English poetic tradition, and came to feel that it was, after all, part of his 'voice-right'.

Seamus Heaney's most recent 'act of translation', Robert Henryson's *The Testament of Cresseid & Seven Fables,* has an entirely different character.

Heaney has written feelingly of his sense of an 'intimacy' between himself and the late fifteenth-century Scottish 'maker'. The intimacy goes deep, but is felt most immediately at the level of language, or, more specifically, a shared dialect, as Heaney explains in *The Guardian* of 30 May 2009:

> The work was enjoyable because Henryson's language led me back into what might be called 'the hidden Scotland' at the back of my own ear. The speech I grew up with in mid-Ulster carried more than a trace of Scottish vocabulary, and as a youngster I was familiar with Ulster Scots idioms and pronunciations across the river Bann in Co Antrim. I was therefore entirely at home with Henryson's 'sound of sense'...

A pointed instance of Heaney's delight in their shared *lingua franca* is to be found in his remark in the same article to the effect that what started him on the translation of Henryson was the 'jaunty, canty note' which he found at the opening of the first of Henryson's 'moral fables', 'The Cock and the Jasp'.

With respect to Weinberger's first principle for translation – *advocacy* – Heaney has written of his wish to bring Henryson's work out of the rarified world of university halls and into the public domain, to render it more accessible. At the same time, he acknowledges that the Scots language of the originals is 'not very difficult'. The resulting volume, with its text and facing translation, is therefore one in which Heaney's version functions not so much as a crib but as a rather delightful variation on the original fifteenth-century texts – a volume which allows and even invites the reader to skip from right to left, from Heaney to Henryson, and back again. In this way, we may perceive with pleasure both the skill with which Heaney retains the difficult rhyme royal verse which Henryson himself carried over from Chaucer, as well as the subtle differences in syntax and nuanced word-choices made by Heaney, which appear as so many 'grace-notes' to augment the musicality of Henryson's narrative voice. Indeed, so great was Heaney's own pleasure as he worked through this translation that he says he often felt tempted 'to hum along'.

But of course, it would be a mistake to suppose that Heaney's admiration for, and consequent advocacy of, the work of Henryson was confined to certain linguistic and formal affinities. Heaney states in his Introduction that the Scots poet 'is a narrative poet whom you read not only for the story but for the melody of understanding in the storytelling voice'. And again: 'If his rhetoric is elevated, his sounding line nevertheless goes deep'. Like Heaney, Henryson is a poet for whom word and meaning are but two halves of a whole; hence, the Ulster poet's profound appreciation of what he calls 'the sound of sense'.

Finally, in respect of Heaney's view of Henryson, one might note that they share a fundamentally 'moral' – but not moralistic – view of the world, one tempered for both by a generosity which recognises the difficulties of life and is forgiving of many of man's errors. Indeed, when Heaney says that Hugh MacDiarmid would have found in the work of Henryson 'the poetry of a grown man', he might equally be referring to himself. The intimacy between these two authors runs deep.

I

Enough has been said to establish what Heaney felt was 'here' for him in the works of Henryson, and inclined him to translate two of his chief works as an act of 'advocacy'. However, the *Testament of Cresseid* is unique among the poems chosen by Seamus Heaney for translation, insofar as it cannot stand on its own, as a 'discrete' poem. For it was, of course, written as a 'response' to Chaucer's *Troilus and Criseyde*. At this point, it is difficult not to be reminded of T S Eliot's famous essay, 'Tradition and the Individual Talent'. Because Henryson's poem engages at such a profound level, and in such a nuanced way, with Chaucer's *Troilus*, one cannot (to use Eliot's terms) comprehend the 'complete meaning' of the former without reference to the latter.

The many fifteenth-century works written in 'the Chaucerian tradition', while they used to be regarded as relentlessly dull and inferior imitations, are now recognised to relate to the courtly works of Chaucer in subtle and well-informed ways; they are seen to 'insinuate' oblique and extraordinarily delicate interpretations of Chaucer's most enigmatic works into their own poems – interpretations which are so brilliant as to remain unmatched by a very few (if any) modern critics. The true nature of these works is suggested by the critic A C Spearing, as follows:

> The kind of skill which nowadays goes into literary criticism went in the Middle Ages...partly into *retellings* [my emphasis] of existing stories in such a way as to incorporate the findings of the writer's critical and interpretative reading of his 'auctors'.

Henryson's *Testament of Cresseid* is a textbook example of a work which participates in and even exemplifies this process of insinuation and discovery.

Heaney's perception that Henryson's *Testament* incorporates a subtle, nuanced, interpretation of one of Chaucer's greatest works can only have added to his feeling that there was indeed something 'here' for him in the *Testament*, and to the urgency of his desire to translate it. However, the very subtlety of Henryson's 'response' to Chaucer's *Troilus*, together with the fact that the modern reader stands at a remove of several centuries from both these poets, necessitated the rather extraordinary 'translation-strategy' which Heaney adopts here, which is at once complex and self-effacing. It was no part of Heaney's purpose here to achieve any kind of 'mastery', still less to claim a 'voice-right'. Instead, his task – as he conceived of and brilliantly accomplished it – was firstly to respect Henryson's own profound 'sound of sense', and secondly to perform what Heaney himself describes (in a quite astonishing turn of phrase) as 'sense-clearing'.

We are not left to speculate as to the precise nature of this dual strategy for very long. Within a mere four lines of its opening, Heaney gives us a hugely suggestive 'clue' as to what his *modus operandi* as translator of the *Testament* will be.

Henryson's opening goes as follows:

> Ane doolie sessoun to ane cairfull dyte
> Suld correspond and be equivalent:
> Richt sa it wes quhen I began to wryte
> This tragedie...

Heaney's facing translation reads, startlingly:

> A gloomy time, a poem full of hurt
> Should correspond and be equivalent.
> Just so it was when I began my work
> On this retelling, …

Heaney's translation here, insofar as it not only obscures but entirely 'deletes' Henryson's important reference to his work as a 'tragedie', is extremely odd and discomfiting. It appears clumsy, and ignorant of the decorum of translation. For while the 'real' Seamus Heaney is indeed presenting us here with his 'retelling' of a fifteenth-century poem, he allows that 'real' voice, which ought to have remained outside of the text, to intrude, almost to the point of violence, on the voice of the 'translator'. This apparent 'mistranslation' is heightened in an ironic way in Heaney's Introduction to this volume. There, he discusses with consummate skill his translation of these first four lines, speaking in considerable detail about their 'phonetic make-up', including his attempt to replicate the force of the Scottish 'r's in 'cairfull' and 'correspond' and (especially) 'tragedie'. Here, I suggest, Heaney is speaking in his most 'jaunty, canty' tone. Far from being the work of a dullard, this passage actually 'flags up' what will be the two essential elements of his translation-strategy in the *Testament*. Firstly, and because he so much wishes the original voice of the Scots poet to be heard by a modern audience, he will, as he says, 'keep the accent' of that original. Secondly, Heaney's seemingly bizarre translation here ought to alert us to the fact that, at those moments when he feels that the modern reader, by virtue of a huge temporal gulf, may be precluded from hearing the important 'undermusic' of Henryson's narrative voice, he will indeed intrude an obtrusive or seemingly inappropriate word or phrase into his otherwise harmonious 'retelling', in the expectation that we will be made to pause and puzzle over the incongruity – perhaps even getting out our dictionaries – in order to fathom and fully understand moments of particular enigma and/or revelation in Henryson's 'coded book'.

II

In his translation of the *Testament*, Heaney for the most part trusts to Henryson's own 'sound of sense', and is content simply to keep the accent of his source text. However, as the interpretative enigmas deepen, towards the end of the *Testament*, Heaney makes a series of brilliant and bold lexical choices which serve to point up and alert his readers to important subtleties in Henryson's text which we might otherwise have missed.

A significant degree of refreshment – in the sense of making visible something which had been opaque – is evident at several places in Heaney's translation. For example, he chooses to render Henryson's 'almes' as 'charity'. And he also translates 'humanitie' as 'charity'. Henryson uses the term only once, in the final stanza, where it is replicated by Heaney. This suggests that Heaney wishes to point up the fact that – in the minds of many readers and critics of Chaucer's poems – the tragedy of Troilus is brought about by a hopeless confusion between human and divine love: *cupiditas* and *caritas*.

Again, there is a very affecting scene at the end of the *Testament* where Henryson has Cresseid describe to Troilus her great misery – what Henryson calls her 'greit infirmitie, / Hir legacie and lamentatioun'. Heaney renders this as 'her ordeal, her keen, her testament'. However, at the beginning of the stanza, he interpolates a phrase that is entirely absent from Henryson, but which has huge significance in Chaucer:

> When he had listened to the whole story...

Now it may be simply that Heaney is adverting to the fact that Chaucer had left the story of *Troilus and Criseyde* without making it 'whole'. However, there is more here. Chaucer's preoccupation with telling 'hool' stories goes right back to his earliest work, *The Book of the Duchess*, where he leads us to understand that, in terms of a love-story, many books, including the *Aeneid*, are merely half-texts and do not tell 'the whole story'. Specifically in relation to the *Troilus*, Chaucer becomes dismayed and almost defeated by the fact that the 'olde bokys', on which he is relying for not only the plot but the interpretation of Troilus's 'fatal destyne', are not 'whole'. I suggest therefore, that the line quoted above is in fact an instance of Heaney working as *vates* or 'seer', demonstrating an exquisitely astute understanding of the problems posed by the *Troilus*, even to Chaucer himself.

But perhaps the most breathtaking example of Heaney's 'sense-clearing', one which works to jolt us into an awareness of a particularly elusive moment of understanding evinced by Henryson, occurs in his translation of the final stanza of the *Testament*. The final three lines of the original address women and read as follows:

> Beir in your mynd this schort conclusioun
> Of fair Cresseid, as I have said befoir.
> Sen scho is deid, I speik of hir no moir.

Heaney's translation goes:

> Bear in mind the final quick declension
> Of fair Cresseid, as I have told it here.
> Since she is dead, I speak of her no more.

The translation here of 'conclusioun' as 'declension' is startling and obtrusive. And it fulfils Heaney's intention that the modern reader examine closely what Henryson is saying to us, by way of interpretation of *Troilus and Criseyde*. Uncertain as to what precisely the word meant, I had recourse to my dictionary and found that 'declension' could indeed have the sense 'declining, descent, deterioration'. However (and as Heaney was certainly aware) the primary register of this word in a modern reader's mind is a grammatical one: classes of nouns are 'declined', in a series of 'cases' (nominative, vocative, etc.). And any schoolboy who has struggled with certain foreign languages might well recall that there are some irregular nouns, some of whose cases are likewise irregular. Henryson's use of the term, 'conclusioun' here was particularly pointed and important, as it relates to Chaucer's *Troilus*. For the whole source of Chaucer's anguish at Troilus's end is his sense that his has not been a simple, regular 'cas' which embodies the logical and divinely ordained workings of the laws of cause and effect; his punishment, as Chaucer is only too keenly aware, is more appropriate to what Aristotle called 'crime' than mere 'error.' Troilus's is therefore an irregular case. Heaney's 'sense-clearing' here allows us to share in the understanding of what is, in fact, one of the chief 'mysteries' embedded in Chaucer's poem.

There is ample evidence that Henryson conceived his *Testament of Cresseid* not simply as an adjunct to Chaucer's great tragedy. Hence, although the two protagonists are of course different, Henryson wished his tragedy to stand as a parallel to that of Chaucer, and also to represent a variation of (and in part at least, an implicit 'corrective' of) his master's work. The primary indication of the impulse towards the creation of a' parallel' text is Henryson's pointed and important reference to the 'fatall destenie' of Cresseid – an obvious echo of Chaucer's declamatory reference to the 'fatal destyne' of Troilus which Chaucer had uttered in the opening line of the final book of his 'litel ...tragedye'. On the other hand, the most fundamental difference between these two poems is that, while Chaucer had struggled to make his fit the definition of tragedy as a fall from grace which was 'caused' directly by sin, Henryson presents us with a different model: that in which tragedy results in a fall from prosperity to adversity 'caused' by the arbitrary turn of events ('Fortune's wheel') and for which no *moralitas* could (or should) be construed. Hence, for example, Henryson's crystal-clear demonstration that Criseyde's tragic fall is not occasioned by her infidelity. For the leprosy which afflicts Cresseid and leads to her death is punishment *not* for any infidelity in love but for blasphemy. Religious texts from the Middle Ages are unambiguous as regards both the sin and the punishment.

Even more pointedly, Henryson tells us that the gods knew *all* of Cresseid's intention before ever she made her complaint to them. Chaucer had asserted throughout the five books of his *Troilus* that it was his special 'purpos' to relate not just *what* happened to Troilus, but *why* it happened. Hence his heroic (if ultimately unedifying) search for the 'cause whi' or final cause of his protagonist's tragedy. Henryson would seem to be impatient with such irritable searching after reasons. Hence, he uses the term 'schort' twice in his final stanza. And in his final line, he says that since Cresseid is dead, he will speak of her no more. In Chaucer's case, the actual death of Troilus occasioned a veritable 'crise', the production of several hundred lines, and the eventual betrayal by Chaucer of the humane ethos of his own poem in favour of a severe, *contemptus mundi* view, so as to preserve some semblance of faith in God's justice.

All of this may seem totally irrelevant to the volume in question here – Heaney's translation of Henryson's *Testament*. Yet I hope it will go some way towards explaining why, from what he writes in the Introduction , it seems that Seamus Heaney (whisper it) 'prefers' Henryson to Chaucer as a poet, or – better, perhaps, and less alarming for all concerned – why Heaney is more partial to the Scotsman. As he puts it: 'Both strike a wholly mature note, but the Scottish poet's is more richly-freighted with "an ample power / to chasten and subdue."'

III

With respect to the *Seven Fables* which follow the *Testament*, Henryson's carrying over of rhyme royal, the verse-form appropriate to matters of high seriousness, from a 'tragedie' to a series of animal fables, serves to heighten Heaney's admiration of the Scots poet. Moreover, who could not admire the way in which Henryson extends the beast-fable genre to a mode of writing which is extraordinary in its breadth as well as its depth. What had, in the Aesopian, and indeed the Augustinian tradition, been mere animals, are allowed to become 'characters', and to develop 'personalities'. Hence the delightful ambiguities which beset the reader of Henryson's *Fables*. In addition, Heaney sees and admires Henryson's equal command of the donnish learning (*trivium* and *quadrivium*, presumably) and the folk-wisdom of the medieval period, as the source of a rich and original way of looking at the world. To take an example of Henryson's parallel vision: just as one of the astrologised deities in the *Testament* is versed in the principles of medieval physiognomy, so too is the mouse in the final fable related by Heaney.

In place of the grimness of the Aesopic tradition, in which the 'morals', such as they are, relate to survival rather than any exercise of virtue, Henryson takes care to associate 'prudence' (strictly speaking, the practical wisdom which would help ensure survival), with divine providence (the etymologies of the two are very similar). However, the sequence of thirteen fables is scrupulously organised by Henryson to exemplify a shift away from narratives in which, for the most part, everyone receives the fate he deserves, towards a world which is dominated by evil and powerful men and – most shocking of all – from which God has increasingly withdrawn.

Each of Henryson's thirteen fables, as they appear in this exquisitely-structured sequence, expresses a different point of view, and relates to the others in ways which range from the near-identical to the diametrically opposed. Of course one can only speculate, but it may be that in his selection of seven of these, Heaney was interested less in the *schema* than in demonstrating – and celebrating – the sheer variety, the extraordinary multiplicity of perspectives on man, and on life and the world, which is to be found in Henryson's fables.

It is surely true to say that the chief purpose of fifteenth-century poetry, both as it responds to the wisdom and profound perplexities of the father of English poetry, and as it fashions in itself a 'new thing', is to illuminate and to enlighten. No wonder then that Robert Henryson preserves the poetic form of greatest seriousness for the animal fable, commonly held to be a source of entertainment and relaxation from the 'hard' contemplation of tragedy and the difficulties of life in general.

Both these works address issues of the highest seriousness. And in relation to the way in which the two apparently very different works may be linked, it might be said if (as I believe) the central focus – the alpha and omega – of Chaucer's *Troilus and Criseyde* is the issue of cause-and-effect (or, to put it another way, 'consequentiality'), then one may see a certain significance in Seamus Heaney's decision to translate the first of

Henryson's fables, 'The Cock and the Jasp', which exemplifies a case where an immoral choice has no consequences; and also the last, 'The Toad and the Mouse', a tale of how an immoral choice can bring fatal consequences. In fact, the *Testament* and the *Seven Fables* seem to me to be linked by a whole web of cross-references (for example, to 'syllogisms' and their 'conclusions', and to 'coded books'). However, given that the late Middle Ages was the period when authors first began to think not only in terms of their own intention in writing, but of the 'intention of the reader' (*intentio lectoris*), then it would seem appropriate to leave the reader of both these texts to tease out and discover the connections between them.

It may well be that the combination of the oblique illumination of the most profound enigmas which Chaucer himself could muster, which Henryson 'practises' in the *Testament*, together with his mature and forgiving humanity, and his ability to take a kaleidoscopic view of life (not unlike that of the *Canterbury Tales*, it must be said) was what led Heaney to state that, in his work, Henryson answers Hugh MacDiarmid's definition of poetry as 'human existence come to life'. Could there be any greater accolade?

The modest appearance of this 'little quair' belies its importance in reclaiming for a modern audience the brilliance of a hitherto obscure fifteenth-century author; and its importance insofar as it marks an entirely new and, from the reader's point of view, totally surprising, 'stepping-stone' on the unique odyssey of Seamus Heaney. One will not find in this act of translation – as one may in the translations of *Sweeney Astray* or *Beowulf* for example, any 'miraculous mix of the poem's original spirit with Heaney's own voice'. Seamus Heaney's primary role here is that of 'translator as enabler' – specifically, an enabler of the understanding of a multivocal and enigmatic literary text. And it may be salutary to remind ourselves here that, as Bernard O'Donoghue has pointed out, Seamus Heaney has, from early in his career, 'been recognised as a major critic as well as poet, in the tradition of artist-commentators from Sidney to Coleridge to Eliot. What has dawned on us more slowly is that he is also – to borrow a phrase used to describe Chaucer – a great translator.' It should therefore come as no surprise to find that there is a particularly 'snug' fit between Heaney and Robert Henryson, poet, translator and fellow-interpreter of 'coded books'.

Sean O'Brien

STEPPING OUT

Dennis O' Driscoll, *Stepping Stones: Conversations with Seamus Heaney* (Faber and Faber, 2008), £22.50.
Rand Brandes and Michael J Durkan, *Seamus Heaney: A Bibliography* 1959-2003 (Faber and Faber, 2008), £50 hb.

Seamus Heaney once wrote that the work of Dante seems to come written on official paper: *Stepping Stones* has something of the official communiqué about it, with Dennis O'Driscoll acting as ADC to the project while having actually conceived it himself. O'Driscoll has the wonderful gift of being relentlessly curious (he more or less gets Heaney to draw a plan of the farmhouse at Mossbawn, for example) and at the same time extremely tactful, seeming to enable the poet to answer frankly without feeling put on the spot. Even if it were dull, the resulting very large book would be an invaluable source of reference, but in fact it's a never-less-than-fascinating series of edited and polished conversations for the page, in which the voice of the poet can be heard moving among the life and the work, occupying its familiar range from down-to-earthness to exalted eloquence. *Stepping Stones* amounts to the literary autobiography of a poet with too much on hand to undertake the job himself.

Perhaps for the reader outside Ireland in particular, there is special interest in the description of the complex give-and-take Heaney witnessed between Catholic and Protestant neighbours in his locality, matched with a larger sense of the (at times quite subtle) enforcement of secondary status on Catholics by the dominant Protestant class. Having a strong sense of the anecdote, Heaney more or less forbears to comment on the description of the Twelfth of July by his editor at Faber, the Ulsterman Charles Monteith, as a 'Fine old folk festival'. If Heaney were given to such formulations, this would be a fine example of Althusser's description of ideology as the gap between what people need to think is there and what there really is. And again, though Heaney would be unlikely to speak of it in such terms, his own success has been a version of what in the case of Tony Harrison and Douglas Dunn has been called 'the scholarship boy's revenge'.

Throughout these well-tuned conversations, Heaney serves his remarkable gift for vivid summary, seeking always to give the sense of experience as an event rather than something over and done with – cattle running up the ramp of a lorry, an encounter with Danny Morrison on a train, the pleasure of stacking hay and the pleasures of reading such vastly different poets as Hughes and Larkin and Walcott, whose work seems to materialise before us as he evokes it. He tells it all as he believes it to have been, from early childhood to his position now as a seventy-year-old smiling public man, and the centre of all his concern, to which the book is forever returning one way or another, is the effort to balance the liberty of art with its obligations. To readers grimly accustomed to the miserable parsimony, sulphurous jealousy and pathetic snobbery with which literary affairs are often conducted, it's a relief to be reminded that poetry is a fit occupation for grown-ups.

Not that Heaney is wholly immune to the odd glint of resentment himself. To be otherwise would be inhuman. For example, his handling of the various missiles hurled his way by A Alvarez is deft and extremely funny, embodying what John McGahern called 'implacable courtesy'. Asked to recall Alvarez's unfavourable review of *Door into the Dark*, Heaney comments: '…in fairness it's as well to remember that Alvarez had been part of the action when Sylvia Plath and Ted Hughes were getting going a few years earlier; since my stuff came in the wake of all that, he probably felt that everybody needed to be reminded of it. Alvarez thinks of himself as a poet, of course…'

The point Heaney doesn't pursue is that to Oxbridge-London literary types of Alvarez's generation the idea of an Irish poet from a modest rural background rising to eminence might well have seemed a denial of the rules of the universe. Ireland and the Irish forty years ago were certainly not regarded in the same way as they are now, as anyone growing up then in Britain with an Irish name could testify. Those writers nearer to Heaney's age – Douglas Dunn, for example – had a better understanding of the matter, knowing that class and nationality mattered more than was publicly admitted, while subsequent generations of poets in the UK would look to Heaney and Derek Mahon for immediate poetic examples. Nothing is as dead as a defunct orthodoxy, and though it isn't mentioned here, it must have been galling to some to find the likes of Lowell and Hughes enjoying warm and mutually admiring relations with the newcomer.

Does any of this stuff matter? Probably not in the light of eternity, but it's part of the context in which we see Heaney's body of work taking shape, something against which he must, in a favourite term, have 'braced' himself, for example by recalling Pound's view that the opinions of those who have not themselves done 'distinguished work' are not to be taken seriously. It's a position that quite late on in the book requires him to enlist Helen Vendler as a critic who thinks like a poet, but presumably the whole point of exceptions is that they are exceptional. More important is the way Heaney employs an example from visual art to emphasise his conviction that the aesthetic and the moral are of a piece, and that, at the same time, the idea that this is so cannot be permitted to become merely one more position taken for granted. Discussing his poem 'To a Dutch Potter in Ireland', about Sonja Landweer, whose father was murdered by the retreating Nazis, he recalls her description of swimming among the phosphorescent plankton of the Norder Zee: 'Sonja was marked by the cruelty and evil of what happened to her father, but also by the beauty and marvel of what happened to her on that shore, so she has a profound sense of what is at stake in the making of art…She has fierce conviction about the value and necessity of good and beautiful work – as well as a horror of work where she detects the spirit of nihilism.'

It is of course wholly natural and proper that Heaney should discuss art in these terms, but reading these comments and others reminds me of the more dismal discourse that seemed in prospect when, after he'd won the 2007 T S Eliot prize for *District and Circle* he spoke from Dublin, while still recuperating from illness, to the BBC Radio 4 *Today* programme, fronted that morning by the unfailingly contentious John Humphreys. Humphreys began by asking him why *District and Circle* was not a more angry book, since poets were supposed to be angry, weren't they? Courtesy is a conspicuous feature of Heaney's work, but the idea was clearly too complicated for the occasion – yet another of those times when, in Britain at any rate, an opportunity to consider the value (the necessity) of poetry is not so much blown as completely unrecognised.

The BBC has recently undertaken to show the public 'why poetry matters'. They could have done a lot worse than put up numerous quotations from *Stepping Stones* on the website. The banal, instrumental view of language held (often both unwittingly and aggressively) by journalists and many others, is shaped by and contributes to what Heaney refers to as the 'dematerialization of language'. For such an audience, Heaney's description of poetry as 'a comprehension which has to be its own reward' may well seem like an attempt to pull the wool over the eyes of dwellers in what is known as 'the real world', but the usual alternative approach, through ingratiating simplification, is a sin against the tongue. Heaney's English detractors, such as A N Wilson, who makes the risible claim that Betjeman is by far the finer poet, certainly look shrivelled and dry in comparison, lacking Heaney's sense of the physicality of language or the dramatic character of verse-music.

As is well known, there is a part of Heaney himself that shares his farming relatives' and neighbours' conviction that poetry is not the be all and the end all, but in him this seems to manifest itself as a refusal of that automatic piety, that settling for habit, to which poets and readers are sometimes prone. He conceives poetry in terms of action, process and event, and he never tires (and nor will the reader) of accepting the lure of 'phonetic purchase or rhythmical promise', trying to edge closer to capturing for the space of a line or a sentence what is of course not finally to be captured.

A recurrent theme in *Stepping Stones* is the challenge of finding time and space to write without distraction while being a husband and father and having to make a living. The economic burden has probably been lifted, but even at his busiest Heaney seems to have kept his head down, and then some. A beautiful book in its own way, *Seamus Heaney: A Bibliography* 1959-2003, by Rand Brandes and Michael J Durkan, lists some 1,240 items – poems, reviews, essays, broadsides and cards, interviews, translations and (always fascinating) ephemera.

Iggy McGovern

TO THE POET ON HIS BIRTHDAY

Seventy years, a growing up with words
Thran signifiers, slippery Lough eels
Enclose them and they scatter as wild birds
Porous, like water-carrying in creels.
Poet, you coax them back out of the air
Indented in the forge's dusty heat
No lantern-bearing seeker takes such care
Getting them true, each time, the knowing beat.

So! Take the day off, leave aside the pen
The chair, the desk, the blotter and the page
Open the skylight, give rein to the tongue...
North-south, east-west, from hallowed hall to fen
Eschew the people's call to 'act your age':
Seventy years a-growing – ever young!

Edward Jarvis

RIB

for Nathan

The coyote rib is broken, halved
and no more than the length
of a palm and open fingered hand.
It contained a thousand thousand
breaths. I found it
in the shallows of a Sierra stream,
meat bleached away, where there was
marrow, a hollow straw. Holding it
a ceremony of howls is loosed as the wind,
giving voice to aspen,
a whisper to the firs, this cold
bite to my stubbled face.

D Nurkse

BRIEF SHOWERS IN THE FOOTHILLS

Loving another person, she says, is like dying in your sleep,
it is impossible, or it can happen only in the past
where there is no self to distinguish, no grey green pine
against which to see the rain: in a dream once, she says,
we died and were walking a mountain road at Finge,
I wore my white dress, you had a thistle in your teeth,
the small dog bounded beside us, sniffing a gentian suspiciously,
and we could tell it was the past only by the mica glint
of a small blue stone we kicked between us.

D Nurkse

INHUMAN LOVE

We created two small lovers, to suffer for us,
and a smaller pair, to console and negotiate,
and many minute ones, to temper that rapture –
they were underfoot always, they adored each other,
sometimes in a paroxysm they nipped our ankles,
or clambered into our laps and searched our pockets
for a pencil, to write another bitter sonnet
we would have to admire, and they too created surrogates,
for the pain of love is too cruel for the self alone,
love makes the mind utterly naked, so the day passed,
our huge steps, going to work, returning, arguing,
reconciling, the click of tiny keys, recording.

Dawn Wood

COMPARISON OF A FRENCH BULLDOG WITH THE 15,000-YEAR-OLD BONE OF A BISON

The junk-shop assistant, in mauve, has sprung
from a Beryl Cook. I am waiting to pay
for the bone of a bison, but she is cradling Louis, a bulldog.

A couple are debating if this variety would suit them –
the man of the couple nudges me: firstly
to mention that the eyes of the breed

are its Achilles' heel, are prone to popping out,
and secondly, because of my accent,
to say that he used to live in Donaghadee.

The vertebra nestles between my thumb and fingers,
warm as onyx, but porous: alive in a sense
that it has forgotten what it is to be vulnerable,

though a skelf chips and falls
to be indistinguishable from the dust.
The wife is paying just enough attention

to let me know that the nudge means nothing,
she sees, indeed, that I know it is nothing,
she relaxes: *such bat ears! such a Winston Churchill face!*

The price tag has been edged with pinking shears:
pink and blotted, it looks older than the bone.
The owner of the dog, a burly guy, is lapping up

praise, is in no rush, but still, this is dallying.
The bone is curled in its own warmth.
From that perspective we are all goners.

Dawn Wood

EYE OF THE HEDGEHOG

Patient in his 'died and gone to heaven' pose,
that berry-eyed glint of such intelligence
is in actual fact a composition involving the mirror image
of two fluorescent striplights, poised to converge,
and a square of window out to Constitution Terrace,
where the roadworks' drilling is threatening to agitate
the boxed moths upstairs from their wings,
to startle, on this level, the doll-like pupil
from where she haunts the centre of the eye
of every once-live thing.

Dawn Wood

ON THE NATURAL HISTORY OF PIPISTRELLES

They are practically only skins,
habit-hooked to twig-bone.
They wear fluff on their sleeves.

They are found in hawthorn bushes and thickets,
but they've also been sighted out in the Atlantic,
and caught in the slipstream of windmills.

As I cycle on Station Road, they have flown
with me for minutes. Am I dishevelling food?
Are we a tunnel of slight heat before the T-junction?

They will knot themselves to the bolt
of a white handkerchief if I wave
it at the back door at twilight.

They have the tiniest of teeth
in a snarl of a mouth. They devour
the presence of swallows and sparrows.

Mary O'Donnell

GARAGE EVENTS

Where you hid the letters
beneath the gas cylinder,
where once you both restored
a desk, rushing to the blonde wood
panels, the green leather surface
a lake lean with light
from the evening sun,
forgiving as you swam together
in the ease of doing.
Where you also found a rat
in a potato-barrel, mistaking it
for a large mouse,
your fingers hooked gently
beneath the heart-bobbing belly.
You lifted it free, noting
the long, ringed tail,
the cosmology of those unblinking,
brown eyes. Small rat,
small rat, surprised – shocked –
did not bite, but hung there,
a minky curve in the O
of thumb and finger.
You lowered it to the wood pile.
It paused, then slipped silently
within catacombs of dried birch,
poplar, safe in the dark.

Paul Perry

WHATEVER

Back then you were full of impetuous
passion, all or nothing promises,
like the hot Mediterranean sun in July.
Said things like now or never.

Words were like drums.
And you climbed all the trees.
Painted your face
and tried to fly a thousand times.

Clover and honeysuckle
you tangled in and drank.
Chickadees chirped for you
and the nights conspired.

Somewhere in the haze,
the drop-zone addiction
of the now said stop and the fields
once green grew overgrown.

The self remaindered itself,
met its image in a cul-de-sac
of confession and retreated
to a place without adjectives.

Not that it started you praying,
but it did make you a little blind.
Your handwriting grew large
enough to make out but not understand.

Now you make love to any man
with an echo of the 'only you'.
You forget their names as quickly
as the light goes out

and walk alone by the canal
to where you once lived.
That's what happens.
A life of wrong turns and detours

takes you away from where
you thought you were going.
Blame chance if you like.
Blame youth or the midday sun.

Blame Tantalus and the golden dog.
Whatever. The main thing is to remember
what you once had and pine,
go on, keep crying,

now you're the girl at the circus,
the one without her candy-floss.
Your grey eyes returned me
to where I am. Still bitter,

still mad, but not so dangerous to know,
no? The images you sell, if only
you worshipped them, bang on the doors
of your dreams. There's one

of a violin, or a man playing a violin,
two birds rest on his lap, the music
takes him above the city,
and away from the names

you once gave to their love.

Timothy Shea

GIVING CPR

Not your soul but your head and chest have left us; now their function
is mine.
Speak with me. Come closer. We must be one together –

The dome my hands form is your first box turtle's shell,
and in each of your legs a walk I have yet to take.

You see, right now your body is both here and not here, accountant
and ghost.
And right now you only have me, this crowd of onlookers
and the crowd's whispers,
which sound like a bit of the old, cracked speech oozing from the
picture hanging here on the wall.

Sleeved in a warped frame is a night shot of the Coney Island
fireworks, 1949.
Somewhere in that scene, my grandfather cradles my newborn
mother
below what looks like white streamers in a black sky, and below
that,
the *ooohs* and *aaahs* of New York swathing the beach
and boardwalk shop windows.

Once, before a shoe store window as distant and smudged as those
in this photograph, I saw a young man slide his chin, slowly,
from one shoulder to the other,
then press his right hand against the glass, and collapse.

His girlfriend calling for help, she must have felt so far from him
that night,
surrounded by those who were still up or pouring from the bars,
the street unrolling down to the river and the river out to sea,

where I thought, then, that everything ended, where the moon's
pull and the water's grade
smoothed everything to sand or skipped stone or, right now,
to the foyer's ceramic tile floor your still limbs spill across.

Right now I have only you. Stay with me. Stay and let my hands
  be your lungs,
my panic your blood. Take my breath if only for a cough.

David Sergeant

21ST CENTURY WEST

Each night, above my garden, your new comets
Chatter to each other on their way,
Asleep by their tail-lights, for touch-down by morning
And cocktails on the pavements of LA,

Delhi, Tokyo. Imperial officials
Sat, once, like this, counting wheat in their heads
In lonely desert towns,
Served with mint tea and focaccia bread,

Their eyes cased in black, little machines
For processing the world.
Noon, like a bored director, will cast them
As Gods, ivory palms and thighs of gold,

A logical progression, their skin
Faintly scented with the lusts
Performed on a red divan that morning,
Watched by the hotel's jaded parrots,

Aeschylus as a paunched figurine.
Later they will photograph the desert
And the sea, the endless sea
Of faces will produce a silver teapot.

Each night the comets pass above my head
And I imagine their landing,
It's beautiful, like nuclear blooms walking
Across the earth, on a dark computer screen.

Gerard Lee

STRAY FEATHERS

ROBIN
Rolls out the red carpet
of her breast
to greet the Spring.

HERON
Night-song of rust,
grey glider into dusk.
Slate-patient shallows stalker,
spearing minnows in your reflection.

SPARROW
In a chittering flourish
of unremarkable brown
they skitter round the patio,
plundering crumbs.

MAGPIE
Cackle-haggling for mates,
twenty-three stormed
Winter's bronchial Sycamore.

In March their artless stack
listing, stuck.
April has three stump-tail chicks.

RAVEN
Tattered cow-pat flipper
sticking in your prate.

From Duncan's battlements
your mother caws:

'Wipe that shit off your beak,
we've got visitors.'

Edward O'Dwyer

YOUR LIFE ON THE DOLE

Each day a little more
you're dreading walking by
the window of that *Subway*
finding that, in it,
isn't your most recent ex-girlfriend,
and she isn't still serving greasy sandwiches.
It's once a week now
you're Googling all the names
you can remember
from that little black book you never kept,
making sure your sudden departure
hasn't been the telling factor
in any rapid rises
to fame and fortune.
But you're so sure some day,
and sooner rather than later,
will be the fruition of these fears.
That some day you will not be gasping
with relief at the words
no results found –
no more the reprieve in knowing
they're all still relative nobodies;
just as you left them.

Cate Huguelet

PANACEA

When I'm feeling low I like to think
of going to the barber shop
of saying *take it all off pal*
that's right don't be shy
I want it gone.

I imagine the hum of the clippers,
my breath drawn sharp as they graze my ear,
the tangled strands falling to the linoleum
like a pile of dead butterflies.

The buzzard-faced old men
that hang around the place afternoons
quit their talk of the racing results
to drop their fleshy jaws.
I grin at them in the mirror.
They clear their throats and look away.

When the barber removes my nylon cape and shakes it,
it makes a satisfying sort of snap.
I settle the tab and tip him discreetly and then,

rubbing my magnificent buzz,
I head for home,
whistling all the way.

Padraig Rooney

THE FEVER WARDS

I must be half-asleep in the fever hospital
above the town. Cathedral bells and coughs,
and candles lit beside the winched-up beds
beneath the moon, the northern stars and frost.
The roof is gone and in its place a canopy
of cloth of gold and parasols that flutter
along the path towards the sanatorium.
We're moon bathing and taking in the air
as the fever wards come down around us
in brick dust and granite blocks and spores.
A wrecking ball destroys a stained-glass window
and swings back out as though a pendulum
were marking time across the patchwork fields.
It showers us with glass and shards of lead
and leaves a broken mosaic on the quilt.
We're outside catching breath and watching
the customs huts asleep in their own silence,
the creamery cans that man the ends of lanes,
the polytunnels' darkened mushroom beds.
And on the bedside table a *Lourdes Messenger*,
a thermometer and damson plums from home.
They smell of coal as though they'd taken in
the smoke that used to puff behind the orchard
before the war. The northern trains are gone
and in their place the disused sidings, sleepers
that smell of creosote warming in the sun.
I'd rise and take my folding cot and walk
if only for this fever that shakes me nightly,
all my nerves on stalks like rhubarb leaves
to catch the rain, or gongs announcing dinner
or benediction in the nurses' home.

Winner of the Strokestown International Poetry Competition, 2009

Eamon Grennan

NEAR THING

Wondering why the kingfisher wasn't catching fire
in flight, but making a great racket at the top
of the Norway spruce, I saw a hawk – a marsh hawk –

swoop in on silent wide-open wing and almost snatch
the half-cracked racketeer from its perch
among the green needles, not one of which the hawk

hit as it missed the belted blue-and-white top-knotted
noisemaker, who took off in a flash, a blue-grey flame
lighting up that tree-top space, a stage where these

actors – one all indignodefiant voice, the other
cloaked in lethal silence – played out their drama
of life and death and near-death experience

that's over in under a minute, the marsh hawk
in two big wingbeats gliding away, the kingfisher
climbing high, higher, higher over the drained

campus lake (his kingdom gone), still shouting.

Eamon Grennan

GLOW

The kestrel standing on air, and your own two eyes hovering
over any small creature aching in the arms of its own life,
companion you this afternoon on the walk downhill
to the sight of Renvyle Bay shimmering and simmering
in the glow of the hottest day this summer: the tar
bubbling and glistening, air spilling over with
targlow, dustglow – all the hedges half white with dust.

Somewhere behind and high up, hawk eyes watch over
some little life till the right moment happens, impact
happens, some other knowledge happens. Later
you're restored to the friendship of that mountain ash
sprouting out of a limestone boulder, rowan berries lit
like Hallow'een tapers: each year you're startled
by its rock-rooted life, its unlikely restoration, the glow

of hope it offers: how it shows again what's possible.

Eamon Grennan

SOUL STIRRING

Had the communion chalice been neither gold nor silver
but a cup of fired clay or plain glass the priest would
half fill with wine, to which – from the other cruet, held
in the steady hand-hold of belief – you'd add water,

how different the whole enterprise might have been:
soul still a live bird that *whets and combs its*
silver wings, not dry skin and blanched bones
growing dusty in the locked closet. But even now

the task of bringing body and soul together remains
and won't be gainsaid, thirsty-spirited as we are
and hungry for otherness – knowing flesh itself,
dear as it can be, is not the answer. So you sit

by this early-morning window and contemplate
all those wind-bidden, ceaseless little shiftings
among the sycamore leaves: such delicate touchings
as they're moved from call to response to call,

tip answering quick tip, each touch a small syllable
in the almost endless dialogue of mutual affection,
attention, assurance that *we're all in this together*,
each feeling – as the breeze increases – *a vigour in*

sense/ That was all Spirit, as another day, like and
unlike every other day, starts and they answer to it,
take on its ordinary astonishments: the bread as bread,
the wine mere wine, and all things simply amazing.

Eamon Grennan

WONDERSCAPE WITH COWS

By the light of ditches brimming with meadowsweet, loosestrife,
  montbretia
    and the purple glow of heather, you wonder

what it would sound like if the redbreast that's just dropped down
  near your feet
    or the cow staring over the fence at your staring self

could speak, sharing their sense of the moment. Something you'd
  grasp, maybe,
    or, more likely, they'd sound like Bashō's pheasant

that simply *screeches, seeing the mountain.* Angling away from this,
  you consider
    the rushes where six heifers lie in wait for rain,

and wonder if you'll see them get up slowly, crooking their knees,
  and put their
    solid foreheads to the ground to fashion

one of their shapes for prayer. See the lake? Sky-blue some mornings,
  others
    either the steely sheen of glass, or ruffled

like the wale-ribbing the strand has when the tide withdraws – and
  you wonder
    when the *heavy hand of blessing* will

stroke this still undrinkable water. Meantime, so sited, you follow
  the zigzag that's the wanderlust of the poem

across open country when the weather closes in and the mist starts
  to harden
    into rain and there's nothing for it but to find

your own way down, wondering if that shape glimmering in the distance is
  a break in the cloud or another lake

you'll have to, soaked to the skin, take in the meaning of and trek around.

Eamon Grennan

NOW YOU SEE IT
(after Thomas Kinsella)

A mockingbird deep among the dark green spiky leaves
and bloodred berries of the holly bush eyes me as I pass
into the library where I'll seek among thickets of books
some such perfect moment: soft mass of the bird's back,
the still-open white window of its wing, the bodkin points
of the holly leaves, and that one blood drop of a berry
the bird is about to swallow – that still glints its instant
in the quick, exacting beak, and all the world waiting.

Tony O'Dwyer

REDEMPTION ON STATION ROAD

After the last snow has slipped from the hills I walk up
Station Road to the music of water. Beneath a tangle
Of ferns and clubmoss, a ditch has concealed
An orchestra of winter notes; riffs and chords
In counterpoint to the dead or waiting fields.

In the distance there is the dull thud of nails
Hammered to a roof truss. Someone is building
A house among leaves and now another sound,
Almost like language, comes into being.
Something new is taking shape, words become flesh.

Behind the coldness of a farm gate
A horse stands rooted, grey and low-backed,
As if posing to be cast in bronze and set
In the centre of some grand city square,
Or merely listening to the land's unhurried breathing.

I reach my hand inside the bars to touch the warm skin
Of his forehead. I feel death in the silent bones
Of his skull; the fled soul; the hollow shell
Clothed in the shabby rag of his life. His eyes
Are like almonds, like mine, and beg me to remain.

But I turn to walk back Station Road.
The music follows me like an angel
Or love searching for incarnation.
I gather it into the shape of all that is lost
And carry it home under the early stars.

Heather Craig

THE POET'S TRYST

Taller than a sycamore he stands up the backlight. He sings
gyrsongs about swans and swallows whole planets.

You shake his voice with a grain of sand
sifting through an hourglass.

He can darkle the rhyme, span the syntax with all talk;
watch him cut figure eights on the lawn.

You pick up his walking stick, his old-man hat,
tread that long path.
                                        And he's there,
crumpled pants from bending over flowerbeds,
dirt under his nails. You ask him where you should go
and he answers:
                                        the slow turning of a leaf.

Ana María Sánchez-Arce

TODAY

Today I feel like iron at the blacksmith
heated until I melt, battered into shape.
That is not me (that shouldn't be me).
Hiss in the bucket.
Shivers.
Contraction and withdrawal.
My eyes do not open.
The weight of it.

Ana María Sánchez-Arce

THE SHADOW

I spy on you because I'm bored
with myself. I'm not as interesting
a subject as you are, receive no news,
talk to no one.

I spy on you because you're not bored
with my spying. I know you find it flattering
to be a subject, share your news,
be the substantial one.

Ana María Sánchez-Arce

CLICK

Picking your words
not once in a while,
but every day,
is like being stuck in a minefield,
forever back and forth,
paying attention to your feet, your speed,
choosing the appropriate track…

Pick-pocket of the mouth,
you know the words are not yours but someone else's,
yet you dare go through with it.

The problem is not making contact with the booby-trap –
uttering those words you skilfully collected
and which will let you down.

It comes after you stand in unfamiliar territory,
presume it is conquered
and move on.

Then as your weight shifts,
as your lips part,
you know for a brief moment
the end has come.
You have been found out
and that 'click' reveals
your vulnerable imperfection.

Ana María Sánchez-Arce

TONGUEPICKER

As you speak he listens in,
coveting for himself the foreign sounds.
Watch him carefully and you will notice
his mute lips shaping the way yours did.

He doesn't say,
but this new tongue he's exercising
pushes awkwardly against his teeth.
It is far too big.

So at night, when everyone's asleep,
it fills his mouth: flat, thick,
already anxiously dented
on both sides.

Peter Richardson

LATE RISING TAI CHI

Lie here with me on your side, our right arms saluting the ceiling,
the two of us sighting along the wrinkled skin of our knuckles

at the stucco above our fingertips and, hauling your pillow over,
set up a pendulum-like motion with me, mimicking the stems

of aquatic plants in a storm-tossed lake – exuberant rhizomes
thrusting up pale flowers whose aroma rewards the swimmer

willing to wade through knee-deep muck for a midday dip,
the swimmer with moxie enough to stop and smell the mix

of pepper and liquorice rising from roots in submerged logs
as lightning strikes a tree on a facing slope. Press your belly

and thighs to the back of me and refrain from laughing,
dear, long enough to make your arm the neck of a bittern

whose whole attention is given over to joggling her body
so the upper part of her blends with wind-punched grass.

We'll know whether we want to be live-in flora or fauna,
or visitors cringing at thunderbolts, transients on a dare,

choosing whether to beeline to our clothes or float back
slowly – kicking our heels at the white heads of the lilies,

glad we've ruled out the swifter sensible exit for a taste
of aquatic dawdling where the air crackles with static.

Michelle Cahill

THE GHOST SHIP

I found the man alone, rocking in a ship's hull,
off the island; the winds baffling, a lee current
lifting anchor, purling rain on the grey horizon.

There was an albatross in the cradle of his elbow,
the bird slain. The scent of cold feathers, a musk
pungent as a magnolia, tossed with brine and bilge.

Outside, the moon glimmered in haloes. The ship
was ghost-like, abandoned by its crew, and the eye
of the albatross was a dark crescent, strangely wide.

Waves slapped against the ship's brow as it creaked,
testing the ice floes. Storm petrels cried and faltered.
Perhaps the only other sound was the man's breath.

I lulled him to sleep. I rowed him ashore in a dinghy.
His body heavy as words I could not speak and slight
as a fledgling's neck. Snow fell thickly where we lay.

But it was hardly a man's form I touched, it was more
like an iris, purple veined, intricate. I might have
milked his sepals for nectar, or swallowed his dreams.

I might have promised him lovely things; an ice
petrel's wing, a green, glassy wave, or a few beads
of amber as daylight broke and he rose from sleep.

The moon had crept away from the shore into oblivion.
The man was deafened, so he said, by whale song,
a warble, as loud as the chaos of a children's playground.

Take me back to the ship, he implored with politeness
and cowed rage, and the moment that he uttered these words
I saw the vessel, pitching in a storm, in colossal waves.

Soon the man was in his cabin, spellbound by the song
of lost leviathans, the smell of brine, bilge, and burning oil.
Birds circled the grey skies, but there was no white albatross.

And now, when I look from the shore, I see no ghost ship
for the snow is falling like a bitter hymn. Sometimes I think
I see the baleen whales spout a fine spray, as they rise, sighing.

Desmond Graham

ONE FOR SORROW

Where the bridge
meets nothing
at both ends

and the baronial towers
are hem-stitched
with razor wire

and the long drive
begins its overture
with dogs

in a room
not yet finished
a not quite abandoned

third wife
counts magpies
each morning

just to be sure
there's not only one

Desmond Graham

LAPWING

Does the peewit's twisting
unpredictable flight
show the shapes of wind
even on a calm day

does it show the shapes of danger
it misses
though no danger we can see
is there

does it show
that freedom
is making use of it
lest the air fill up

or the field edge
turn without warning
to wire

Howard Wright

O SLIGO

The cement floor of Hargadons pulls in
gaudy Americans for the dog-collar pint
and sawdust snug, the bench-top spills
and weekend supplements. It's not so much
themed as dreamed, service with a shrug.

*

The unlined car park at the Glenfarne
Ballroom of Romance is more inviting than sad.
The swags of bulbs, the grey tarmac,
are all worthy of a photograph, as is the oldest
Queen of Country who is almost sold out.

*

An acerbic, yet accurate, seagull
highlights the sculpted quiff of lanky Yeats.
The ragged road to the north takes you
to Ballyshannon or Belcoo; crows
and critics and the discomforts of Lissadell.

*

Within sight of the Innisfree Lounge, a boy
and girl in contention on a mid-town bridge,
taunting with spoonbait the rollicking,
writhing Garavogue dragon, and dredging
God knows what from its unconscious.

*

There is but one road in and one road out.
A single dusty second-hander has shelf space
for *Speak, Memory* by Nabokov.
You would rather it had no tongue,
or, like the road, it's best kept in your head.

James J McAuley

INTERIOR WITH A FRAMED PORTRAIT

Despite the lively fire she is gazing into,
The room is chilly. She gathers the fur rug
Round her knees. The frame with its portrait
Sits behind her on the piano, regarding her
Whenever she plays the simple tunes
The old nun taught her when a child herself.
This boy with round cheeks, round eyes
Taking in the rich world beyond the lens –
Their story unfolds from his wide-eyed surmise.

Still, the portrait holds secrets: its pride
Of place, its wrought silver frame a vessel
For emotions stronger than the pang
That his misgivings could muster when he came
To play the role of brother and she of sister; though
Others told tales of a darker kind. Almost from
The cradle, he was thought a *wünderkind*,
But his life, confused and secretive, became
Exciting and disastrous as a shooting star.

No villain, though. His visits were disguised
By versions that could be true. Is this her brother
Enshrined in her drawing-room? Or her child,
Fathered by that fair-haired lazy war-hero
Who courted her briefly, then went to die in action
At El Alamein? At any rate, the photograph
Reminds her to yield to the luxury of grief.

What became of the child? No one can say.
A clock pulses. Embers whisper. She keeps
Their secret safe in its elaborate silver frame.

Jennifer Compton

CRUNCH

Syringes are not scattered
on doorsteps or in gutters
the disaffected in this city
are on methamphetamine.

Or p – which is the pure form
a cruel and unusual lotusland
a species of euphoric violence
invincible lack of consequence.

Junkies nod off. In the fortress
of a fix. They drop their fits from
nerveless hands – you can track
the users through the streets. But

heroin has the Mahatma effect.
And those with darkened eyes
the amok-runners with a kris
the beserkers of the Norse

who ritualised bog myrtle for
their trance of fury have their
descendants here – and now
seek to transcend deep shame.

Ryan Dennis

THE WORDS OF A FARMER ON MONDAY

It is the commerce of farmers with hands in their pockets.
It is used by old wives
and the things they've known not having.
The stains in his pants are scattered language,
and scars the marks of punctuation.
To speak he must harvest the fields for syllables
and the cries of calves for meaning.

The things he says become the atmosphere
that romances the clover each rain.
They fill the woodchuck holes
to save the haybine from trial.

The radio does its best in the absence of terms.
Sometimes cows are lonely things to sing to.

Talk of spiritual ties to the land,
of wholesome ways of living
and it hurts his ears.
He disappears each time.

In a few words he knows who you are,
and he's reminded who he is.
You both feel sad.

Now that you've met the farmer you know his story.
He has told you in personal algorithm:
He dies, losing his farm, losing his mind,
but to a single morning star
he doesn't give up the words
that have held him this long.

Ryan Dennis

THE WORDS OF A FARMER ON TUESDAY

He walks the morning stars to the barn
to wake cows from their dreams,
full of things he might not say that day.

Sometimes his words collect together like pigeons huddled on rafters.
Sometimes they wear on the inside of his chest,
like dirt alleys in a paddock.

A few words he gives to his wife over coffee
swell into a pragmatic humanity
that glides through the woods
and over the heads of coyotes.

Sometimes his words are like broken haybines.

Finally, he has too many words and must die.
It is too hard for air
to filter through packed sentences in his ribcage.

Silence: he makes his final offering to the world.

'Hell smells like teat dip.'
'Milk 71 in the bucket.'
'I am culled.'

Ryan Dennis

THE WORDS OF A FARMER ON WEDNESDAY

He shouts to get them to their feet.
He curses their sicknesses, their obstinacies, their dead calves, and
their grain costs.
He calls them when he feeds them.
These are sounds that don't make a story.

He pulls on his dirty pants in stiff, difficult motions.
It reminds him his legs are embalmed with teat dip.

He climbs the steps of his death bed
which sounds like a tractor.

He gathers a concluding breath and holds it to contemplate his
endowment.
If he says anything it will be lost in a heavy rattle
that ploughs through commas.
He can only exhale in compliance.

His corpse reseeds the field.

Tom Duddy

THE CAFÉ

The best time here is this
heavenly lull between
elevenses and lunch hour
when I have all to myself
for company the waitress
who cannot stop finessing,
finessing. She repositions
a menu card; she pushes in
a chair; she reassembles
the cruets back into sets
that click smartly together;
she wakes up the flowers
of the day and makes them
stand taller in their vases.
(Only once has she spoken
half-personally to me, though
I didn't catch what she said.
It was the time a hail shower
cascaded out of a violet sky
darkening rapidly over the gables
of Shantalla, blew fiercely
across the car parks, and whacked in
the doors, scattering the menu cards).

Though I always ask for one
coffee – regular, black – she
never presumes to guess.
And so each day is a new day.
Which is as it should be.
There is an understanding
that there is no understanding.
This way it remains a mystery
where one has to go when
one rises up, brow furrowed,
urgently checking the time
as one heads for the cash-desk.
There is some joy – more than
she can know – in dropping

the generous tip, nodding
and smiling and turning
clean away before the coin
stops spinning in the wine-glass.

Katherine Duffy

SILK BURNS

The teacher reiterates:
this is a martial art.
This set, the Eight Pieces of Brocade,
was devised by a general, used to train soldiers.
Over the years it's been mistranslated;
it should read *pull tendons till they break*
and White Crane Flaps its Wings
really means *rip shoulders under arse.*

So those of us who'd like to be
Waving Hands in Clouds,
Gazing Back at the Moon,
Picking Up Needles from the Ocean Floor,
Swimming Like a Dragon
will have to take a rain check.

Words and meaning
are disenchanted lovers
warding each other off.
The teacher scolds. Silk burns,
hissing through my hands.

Tom French

HAVING STAYED UP LATE TO FINISH *THE MEDITATIONS OF MARCUS AURELIUS*, AND NOW UNABLE TO SLEEP, I CONSIDER THE TELETUBBIES

Repetition is their natural form of expression.
One word is repeated all day for the simple pleasure
repeating it affords. They have no word for '*snow*',
'*seaweed*' or '*a cow in heat*'.

They use plain discourse, speak appropriately and without
affectation. The infinite and varying meanings, that depend on
minute alterations in pronunciation and tone, of the expression
'*Eh oh*', reveal greeting and leave-taking as important to them.

Money, taste and rain are alien to them. They are natural
democrats and self-governing. Suggestions for group activity,
when put forward by one, are agreed with by everyone.
They have wiped out imagination, checked desire,

and by extinguishing appetite, arrived at toast.
They are both socialist and Buddhist, having grasped
the importance – simultaneously – of communal ownership
and owning nothing. Their asceticism is humbling.

One possession each – a hat, a ball, a scooter, a handbag –
is their single concession to the 21st century.
Communal living comes easily to them because
no Teletubby covets another Teletubby's body.

They practise walking gently on the earth on tiptoes
on cinder paths. Hence, hills and distance are a source
of greater fascination to them than the visions,
received through antennae, that appear on their bellies.

Distinctions between themselves and television are false ones.
Because they understand that all things from Eternity
are of like forms and come round, they are inclined
to practise running in circles. They are Franciscan.

The rabbits and flowers are unperturbed by them
and none has been crushed underfoot in over one hundred
transmissions. They do what they have in hand
with perfect and simple dignity. They have evolved to the stage

where gender is obsolete, and the fur between their legs
is unbroken due to the permanent feeling of well-being
they experience. The qualities they exhibit are sincerity,
gravity, endurance, contentment with their portion

and a simple life, benevolence, frankness, and freedom
from trifling magnanimity. They are stoic and do not despise
death or the loss of sensation, and are resigned,
because they do not grow old, to the knowledge

they will be forgotten. Living forever holds no terror
for them because the knowledge that they are in hell,
(despite the presence of permanently perfect weather,
absence of crippling mood swings, and unlimited fun),

appears to be inaccessible to them. When they have gone
into oblivion, what persisted among them – perennial
astroturf grazed by giant rabbits, and an unnatural
array of flowers – will continue to persist. In their hell

the face of the sun is the face of a human baby.
When the baby human sun face refuses to shine
there is neither the presence nor the absence of night.
Though innovative as an architectural form,

the Tubbytronic Superdome is unlikely to catch on.
They have produced no great music, novels, poems
or plays to date. It is likely they will produce none.

Tom Hubbard

SWEET, CHANCY AND TRANSIENT

Knute Skinner, *Fifty Years: Poems 1957-2007* (Salmon Poetry, 2007), €15.

'Irish-America' was once a simple phenomenon – though painful for those forced by economics to be part of it. At the turn of the nineteenth century, Irish and American literatures intersected on the manner (and outcomes) of a westward exodus. The novella *Maggie: a Girl of the Streets* (1893) by Stephen Crane, better known for *The Red Badge of Courage*, depicted Irish immigrant life in the slums of New York. Ten years later, George Moore's story, 'Home Sickness' (in *The Untilled Field*) has in common with *Maggie* a character who is a Bowery bartender, though in this case he is one who makes an ill-fated return journey to the old country. When in America, he yearns for Ireland; when in Ireland, he yearns for America. Wherever he is, he'll suffer from home-sickness.

In that sense, then, perhaps it wasn't so simple after all. Nevertheless, literature was concerned with the Irish in America, and hardly at all with Americans in Ireland. By the 1930s, with James T Farrell's *Studs Lonigan* trilogy, the fictional locus moved from New York to Chicago. If Americans did venture transatlantically east, it wasn't for long: Stephen Crane produced a series of 'Irish Notes', essentially journalistic reports to himself, as if he were a collective folks-back-home. Perceptive as they were, they were the work of an outsider, interpreting the West Cork village pub in terms of his own geocultural frame of reference: 'On an old mahogany dresser rows of plates face the distant range, and reflect the red shine of the peat. Smoke which has in it the odour of an American forest fire eddies through the air.'

Then, in 1963, JFK visited Ireland and the special relationship acquired new dimensions. Kennedy joked that if the travel arrangements of their respective forebears had been different, de Valera might have become President of the US, and he (JFK) would have been President of Ireland. It has been suggested that as Ireland became less oppressive for intellectuals and the US became more so, there followed a mini-exodus in the direction opposite to the traditional one. Better for an American poet to find himself among the culchies than among the hicks – especially if the former weren't really culchies after all, but in fact proved supportive of readings or festivals, and with an enthusiasm to rival that of the metropolis, Hibernian or otherwise. It's all a long way from Stephen Crane contemplating the degraded populace of Ballydehob. US-born poets such as Chris Agee, Ivy Bannister, Knute Skinner and Richard Tillinghast are integral to Irish cultural life. The last-named recently produced a full-length collection of essays on his adopted country, *Finding Ireland* (2008). The scale of the new relationship is reflected in UCD's development of its Clinton Institute of American Studies, and of course we should take into account the special impetus of America in the peace process of the North.

For a long time Knute Skinner (b. 1929) was in the fortunate – for him – position of having home / work bases in both countries. As a Professor at Western Washington University, he could draw on the superb seascape visible from his window: it's 'like any perfectly ordinary morning', on which the anything-but-ordinary Bellingham Bay and the San Juan Islands can be celebrated in a poem. 'At Coney Island' is an American counterpart to Rilke's 'Das Karussell', but with added uneasiness about childhood and its passing:

> But I see them today on their runaway merry-go-round,
> inhaling the beach and the buildings, the sea and the sky,
> while their mothers are helplessly standing behind on the ground
> and wringing their hearts in their hands till they've twisted them dry.

On a similar note, 'Our Water Supply' ends with the eminently quotable lines: 'How good the spring water was when we had it – / like life itself, sweet, chancy and transient.' Another grimly grinning conclusion belongs to a much-cited Skinner poem, 'The Cold Irish Earth', set by the Cliffs of Moher near his Irish home (and from where he can look in the direction of his other homeland): 'but down at Healy's cross / the Killaspuglonane graveyard / is wet to the bone.' A bizarre ossuary in Rome – is there an ossuary that *isn't* bizarre? – prompts observations on the contrast between the stacked remains and the nervous tourists ('contractile fibres and sinewy tissues intact') heading for the exit to buy their postcards.

By now there should be enough evidence to support the contention that if there's a spectrum of American poetry with the likes of Emily Dickinson and Robert Frost at one end, and with Walt Whitman and Allen Ginsberg at the other, Knute Skinner veers in the direction of the first pair. In the past I've called this the 'laconic-expansive spectrum'. A 'laconic' such as Skinner, as per Dickinson and Frost, works a seemingly homespun Gothicity which is yet quietly artful in the way it jolts the reader out of the even tenor of pleasant expectations. For example, in 'The Custom of Queens', we might think we're in for a piece of cosily comic verse deploying the stanza form of John Godfrey Saxe's 'The Blind Men and the Elephant' or Lewis Carroll's 'Mad Gardener's Song' ('He thought he saw an elephant'). It's an extended ballad form, i.e. you have an extra two lines over the standard ballad quatrain, with a rhyme scheme *abcbdb*. Skinner's poem, however, has 'down' rhyming with itself, or even and unsettlingly (in stanza 3) with its plural form:

> This tickled her but one may reign
> the other way around.
> No principle applies to queens
> when it comes to going down.
> Queens move in a mysterious way
> and have their ups and downs.

As line 5 suggests, the familiar form is further subverted by weird echoes of familiar poetry: William Cowper ('God moves ...'), Shakespeare's *Antony and Cleopatra* ('They were dying, Egypt, dying') and W S Landor's 'Rose Aylmer' ('Ah what avails the sceptred race'). At this point, if I were more of an academic than I am, I'd be chuntering on about intertextuality. As it is, Skinner's 'The Customs of Queens' serves as a playfully compressed anthology of Great Lines, offering us a mordant take on female regality. And not a cute elephant in sight.

Many of the poems in this retrospective volume are praise-poems to Killaspuglonane, where Skinner has lived (when off-campus) since 1964. Darker tones are never going to be far away in any Skinner poem, but he clearly identifies with the place and its people, enjoys both the rhythms and the quirks of rural Irish life. Two of his most remarkable poems, from the 1960s, juxtapose unassuming Killaspuglonane with the wider world-theatre: LBJ and Vietnam, the assassinations of Martin Luther King and Bobby Kennedy. Twenty years on, one of the poet's American personae muses curtly: 'old Ronnie addressed the nation / He wanted more of my money for the Contras' ('Friday Evening').

'The Sorcerors: a Laotian Tale' leaves one pleading for poetry to recover more of that narrative function which it has lost to prose; similarly it needs to reclaim from drama its deployment of personae. Isn't poetry, after all, a form of theatre? We're not talking, necessarily, of specific 'performance' pieces. It's odd that we often refer to a poet's 'voice' in the singular, as if there weren't a multiplicity of voices potentially available to his or her imagination. Knute Skinner has a whole section where, as he says, 'the characters, including the narrators, are all fictitious.'

Anyone who has taught at an American university will smile wryly at Skinner's references to conveyor-belt courses ('Humanities 309... Humanities 108'), his irreverence towards po-faced academic bureaucracy. I recalled the remark of a Connecticut English Dept colleague, after we'd attended a performance of Mahler's 9th: 'That was worth far more than any number of MLA conferences.' Brian Arkins's admirable introduction, interestingly, claims Knute Skinner as a 'Southern poet' in the

Irish sense; usually, when we hear that phrase, we think of Carolina rather than Clare. It's a measure of Skinner's shrewd adoptions and adaptations. To keep it fresh, Irish craziness requires an infusion of American craziness. Knute Skinner duly obliges.

Peter Denman

THE EVENNESS OF EXCELLENCE

George Szirtes, *New and Collected Poems* (Bloodaxe, 2008), £15.

George Szirtes must now be regarded as one of the major contemporary English poets. His reputation has increased steadily over the past three decades, and has been built on a sustained technical mastery, an eclecticism in terms of artistic reference and material, and sheer productivity. All these features are on view in his *New and Collected Poems*, which is a large slab of a book, containing about 500 poems in as many pages. The new poems included here are the last forty-three, post-dating *Reel* (Bloodaxe, 2004), which confirmed his recognition by winning the T S Eliot prize. These new poems are all short pieces, and the longer recent work is to appear in his next collection, due imminently.

In looking at his collections of the past thirty years, Szirtes has chosen to include practically everything, with the exception of translations. There is a strong architectonic sense. This is apparent in the careful arrangement of his books – or rearrangement, as when in *The Budapest File* (2000) he extracted from previous collections works relating to the return to his native Hungary. His first visit back was made in 1984, twenty-eight years after he and his family fled the country when he was eight years old. A strong formal emphasis is also to be seen in individual poems. There are many variations on the sonnet structure, sometimes using the sonnet to serve as a stanza form or verse paragraph unit in a longer poem. He also favours the use of *terza rima* and tercets. The early poem 'An Illustrated Alphabet' moves letter by letter through their sounds. A more recent piece, 'Decades', experiments with epigrammatic quatrains strung together, using references to other poets or to paintings with a grimly sardonic tone, as in the following spin on lines by George Herbert:

> When God at first made man
> Having a glass of blessings standing by
> It seemed a good idea and, after all,
> It does behove a deity to try.

Any discussion of Szirtes's poetry must include a mention of his transnational outreach to Hungary. But his poetry is remarkably English, as he himself avowed in his interview with Isabelle Cartwright in *PIR* 35. It seems to ground itself in the formal and temperamental observances of Thomas Hardy. If the 1950s Movement had matured as a poetic style, grown out of its self-limiting attitudes and arrested development, this is how it might have developed.

George Szirtes has been a frequent visitor to Ireland over the past two decades, including a residency at Trinity College. This has left traces in the several dedications to Irish poets and academics, but otherwise Ireland scarcely figures in his work. This may seem a provincial comment, but it is worth remarking upon in that many of Szirtes's poems are rooted in observations of lived experience, and topographical and geographical particulars abound in his work. Then one realises that there is a selective concentration on England and Hungary, with the two countries set in balance one against the other. Together they provide a mutually constructive set of opposites, each a kicking-off place for exploration of the other. The poems in *An English Apocalypse* (2001) assert the assimilation of Englishness with ferocious irony, riffing on names of places – football grounds, market towns, the Yorkshire moors. And images of the sea abound, as if pointing the contrast between island Britain and land-locked Hungary. In 'Death by Deluge', he imagines the North Sea sweeping across East Anglia where he has made his home, wiping away the place-names and the places until 'all was water-colour', and all that is left is 'less earth than you could shift with a spatula'.

And as the imagery of those concluding lines remind us, underpinning the work throughout is a painterly vision – not just in its choice of subjects, or its emphasis on shape and colour, but also in the sketch-like manner of many of his poems. These sketch-poems may seem incidental, but they are technically adroit and are finished poems, not roughs. The observational quality goes well beyond simple record. The moments are privileged not just because they are selected, but also because they are shaped into a formal composition. This technique emerged early, as in 'The Slant Door', which reads as an expansion of the visual methods of William Carlos Williams's 'The Red Wheelbarrow'.

Szirtes's poems are personal, but not very revealing; the gaze is outwards, towards the shapes and colours discernible in the world, or towards the fractured lines of the history that contributed to his making.

> Everywhere men think and gather. The fields
> make chomping noises in the mud. Harvesters and reapers
> with stoical expressions remark on weather that yields
> a good crop. Elsewhere other croppings. Our keepers
> keep us as we keep our horses, on a tight rein.
> Our horses have mad eyes, but we are sane.

This is the concluding sestet of 'Horse Painter', which takes the form of a double sonnet, and reveals something of Szirtes's manner. The first half of the poem is spoken by the painter (George Stubbs perhaps) and describes the people and, more so, the horses that figure in his paintings: 'It is', as he says, 'my privilege / to lay them bare with a scalpel's edge.' The first person is used sparingly; the concentration is on mediating what is seen. The second sonnet-half stands back and speaks impersonally, punctuated by gnomic generalities that avoid the blandness of generalisation: 'Earth is nature but landscape is property'; 'Nothing is as calm as it appears'.

This *New and Collected Poems* displays the evenness of excellence. Seen *en bloc*, as here, it is clear that Szirtes's work, for all its concentration on observation and history, is in fact an intense journey through the formation of a consciousness, a sort of growth of the poet's mind in reverse. It is not just the uneasiness of history bearing down upon the self that produces these poems; there is also the response to the contingencies that impinge on the poetic awareness.

Michael Cronin

WAYWARDNESS

Ulick O'Connor, *The Kiss: New and Selected Poems and Translations* (Salmon Poetry, 2008), €12.

Ulick O'Connor is known primarily as a dramatist, literary critic and biographer. Although his first volume *Life Styles* was published in 1973 by the Dolmen Press, to be followed by five further collections, his name does not often feature in the agora of poetic remembrance or celebration. *The Kiss*, which includes new and already published poems, is therefore welcome in offering a critical overview of O'Connor's work as a poet. What is immediately striking about the poems gathered here is the ease with which O'Connor moves between private statement and public pronouncement. He clearly has a sense that private and public histories are more porous than the constabulary of fact would have us believe and that poetry can be as much about expressing an uncomfortable political truth as giving voice to the key-hole surgery of jealousy. Yeats is an inescapable presence here, though O'Connor is more tentative, less tempted by the marmoreal self-fashioning of the Public Figure.

One of the consequences of having lived through and extensively studied and commented upon the Irish twentieth century is O'Connor's ability to restore a living presence to the people, both the exalted and the humble, who have shaped the island. In his 'Homage to Sean MacBride' MacBride is presented as both the gifted offspring of a privileged family, magnified by the dual mandate of history and culture, and as the relentless activist, unremittingly ordinary in his daily grapplings with injustice ('In that book-lined room I watched many a night / You finger out a clause, begin the fight / To save some man'). MacBride emerges not as the plaster saint of right-on hagiography but as a man whose past became a resource rather than a burden. The range of intelligent sympathy extends poetically to the world brought to bear on the young O'Connor as he was taken around the Church of the Three Patrons in Rathgar by his nanny, Ann Bell. Even though he can no longer share the piety of his childhood nursemaid his poem has due reverence for the integrity of her belief and the rituals which sustain her living self. Part of the attentiveness to people involves an attentiveness to their practices and contexts. O'Connor tries to capture what is distinctive about both the season and the session. In 'Autumn Scare', for example, he uses the language of menace to define the dramatic flare of an Irish autumn:

But today fear crackled off the crop,
Time has telescoped to make it seem
A week since Fall last fired the trees' top.

Looking to do that most difficult of things, evoke the music of performance in the music of a poem, O'Connor in 'The Piper's Club' wonders what kind of utterance might match the disciplined abandon of the fiddler 'Who saw a blackbird in a gap of light / And trapped its sweetness on a tightened string.' If the early Clarke is somewhere close, it is in part because O'Connor too discovers, through the good offices of the poet and scholar Gerald Murphy, the lyric expressiveness and vernacular energy of writing in Irish. Part of the debt is reciprocated in his rendering of an Irish-language poem by Brendan Behan concerning Oscar Wilde. There is a danger, of course, attendant upon too much informed sympathy – national hubris, Ireland and the Irish as the Chosen Ones. O'Connor is saved from the vaporous self-importance of national myth-making by a robust and combative satirical sense.

In a poem written at the time of the Papal visit to Ireland in 1979 and entitled 'The Department Regrets', the poet excoriates 'our concerned Rulers' who made sure that beggar children were removed by the police from O'Connell Bridge 'Concerned that His Holiness might see / How we Christians love one another.' The chilling title of the poem has an even more disturbing resonance in terms of what we now know about institutional child abuse as practised by Church and State. In 'Easter Week 1986' O'Connor comments on the absence of an official commemoration of the 1916 Rising and the actions of the Gardaí in firing live ammunition over the heads of unarmed demonstrators outside the GPO:

Divided, exhausted, confused spectators
Of an uneasy dawn,
While police fire above the head
Of crowds, for imagined slights,
Their backs turned on that sacrificial shed.
How long before they lower their sights?

On a less despairing and more puckish note, O'Connor in 'One Up' describes how he bested his French rivals for the affections of one of their compatriots intimating that eight hundred years of misery could be turned to good account:

None of her fancy French boys
Could do what I could do

Because they lacked, you see,
Centuries of agony.

O'Connor includes translations of poems by Machado, St John of the Cross and Quasimodo but his literary affections, not unusually for Irish writers of his generation, are first and foremost to France. One of the strongest poems in *The Kiss* is simply entitled 'Marcel' and deals with the last two years of the French writer's life – private obsessions contrasted to the calamitous killing of the Great War – and the uneasy morality of art in an age of slaughter:

He could claim the sheafs beside his bed
Would live, when millions more were dead.

The most substantial engagement with French writing takes the form of translations of eighteen poems from Charles Baudelaire's *Les fleurs du mal* (1857). The translations are ambitious in that they seek to retain the formal music of Baudelaire's writing, particularly the use of end-rhyme. Such attempts can often go disastrously wrong and the annals of literary translation are rich in the grotesquerie of botched attempts at formal equivalence. O'Connor, however, manages on the whole to convey the musical integrity of the verse while not sacrificing sense to the iron laws of the soundboard:

La rue assourdissante autour de moi hurlait.
Longue, mince, en grand deuil, douleur majestueuse,
Une femme passa, d'une main fastueuse
Soulevant, balançant le feston et l'ourlet.
– 'Á UNE PASSANTE'

My ears deafened in the street's mayhem:
A woman in full mourning passes by
Majestic, sad, a languid hand held high,
Lifting and balancing the borders of her hem.
– 'THE PASSERBY'

Baudelaire like Rimbaud and Verlaine has had no shortage of suitors in English but O'Connor's translations are notable for their keen sensitivity to the range of Baudelaire's effects in language. An interest in the possibilities of song is a major contributory factor to the success of the translations, and in compositions of his own such as 'Immortality' or the drama extract 'Lament for Naoise', it is possible to hear again and again the particular harmonies of the sung line. O'Connor, who celebrated his eightieth birthday last year deserves a wide and sympathetic audience for a collection which gathers together the highpoints and heartbreak of a life wholly given up to the waywardness of the word.

Liam Carson

TELLING IT SLANT

Colm Breathnach, *Rogha Dánta* 1991-2006 (Coiscéim, 2008), €10.
Juan Rulfo (Tomás Mac Siomóin a d'aistrigh), *Pedro Páramo* (Coiscéim, 2008), €10.
Muhammad Iqbal (Gabriel Rosenstock a chuir i nGaeilge), *Iqbal: dréachtaí próis is filíochta* (Coiscéim, 2009), €10.
Séamas Cain, *tríd an gcoill* (The Red Jasper, 2008), €10.

Colm Breathnach is a poet of the betwixt and between – one who explores the territories between the past and the present, between Irish and English, and between life and death. And as a lexicographer and terminologist, he is a poet whose concern is to match word with meaning as precisely as possible. His *Rogha Dánta* 1991-2006 trawls through his six collections to date, from *Cantaic an Bhalbháin* to *Chiaroscuro*, and reveals consistent thematic threads – the Irish language itself; his relationship with his father; and the individual's relationship with history, both on a personal level and in a wider national sense. Like many an Irish writer from Seán Ó Riordán to Hugo Hamilton, Breathnach is drawn again and again into 'the speckled territory', and never more so than in the poem 'Trén bhFearann Breac':

> Idir dhá dhath
> idir dhá fhocal
> idir dhá ainm
> idir dhá aigne
> idir dhá áit
> idir dhá theanga
> a chaithim mo shaol
> idir dhá shaol.

'Trén bhFearann Breac' describes the process whereby Irish place-names become anglicised and rendered meaningless. Thus Cill Dara is transmuted into Kildare, Claonadh becomes Clane. Road-signs present the orginal Irish names below the English, and in italic, minimised by the powers-that-be:

> an t-ainm dúchais
> sa chló iodálach
> *claon*insint ar stair na háite

sa chló is lú
faoninsint ag dul ó chlos…

In the word 'claoninsint' (literally 'slant-telling') there is an echo of Emily Dickinson's 'tell all the Truth, but tell it slant'. Thus the poet's journey through Ireland takes on mythic overtones, as he becomes a wandering knight traversing a landscape of castles and queens, forever shifting from the darkness of ignorance to the light of understanding ('téim ón dubh go dtí an geal'). But it is not a journey that has a simple resolution; the poet is hemmed-in ('táim teanntaithe ag ceithearnaigh sa ród'), locked into the space between two tongues ('idir dhá theanga').

Breathnach addresses the Irish language itself in 'A Ghaeilge', just as did Ó Riordán in 'A Theanga Seo Leath-Liom'. Here Irish is personified as a woman with a mercurial personality, alternatively weak and strong, old yet young. It's a poem which deals in oppositions – 'leadhb ar liobarna' and 'fallaing'; 'faobhar' and 'fabhairt'; 'fann' and 'teann'. The result is a poem which enters into the split consciousness of the Irish speaker, alternatively despairing and hopeful.

Breathnach's poetry further deals with the abstractions of language and its attempts to locate the appropriate words for emotion. In 'An Foclóirí' he searches for the words that will best evoke grief:

Cuirim iad ar stór i bhfoclóirí
is liostaí, i gcuimhne ríomhairí

ach níl aon fhocal agam air seo fós.

Cian, uaigneas,
dobrón, dúbhrón
aonaracht,

n'fheadar, aiféala, b'fhéidir.

Níl aon fhocal agam air
as na focail go léir go bpléim leo.

In Breathnach's poetry, grief, death and the lingering psychic presence of previous generations are central. In 'An Fear Marbh' ('The Dead Man'), he personifies his dead father as the Kerry island called 'an fear marbh'. It's a spectral poem, 'ar iomall an chomhfheasa' ('on the edge of consciousness'), charged with allusions to Tír na nÓg and Í Bhreasail. In death, the poet's father becomes an island, set apart from the land of the living:

Ó cailleadh tú, a Fhir Mhairbh
tá tú i d'oileán
sínte ar íor na mara.

Breathnach's poetry, it should be added, has a unique language or lexicon all of its own – one deeply rooted in nature and in the Irish landscape. We have repeated motifs of birds, stones, rocks, islands, rivers, trees, sea, soil and sand. In 'Láchtaint san Otharlann' he compares the rising and falling of a dying man's last breath with the sound of waves. But there is nothing sentimental or fanciful about his writing. The same poem has a stark description of bones beneath skin ('cnámha na láimhe / soiléir faoin gcraiceann'). Breathnach's poems hold their form at all times, they exhibit a calm but confident voice, no matter where they take us – into family memories, jokes, straight storytelling or the mythical realms of Cú Chulainn or Eurydice. Neither is Breathnach afraid to confront feelings at their most extreme – grief, love, loss – and he always does so with great grace.

If Breathnach tries to bring the dead back to life – or at least honour their memory – in his poetry, then Mexican writer Juan Rolfo's novel *Pedro Páramo* quite literally brings them back to life, or some form of life. Rulfo himself described its genesis in a visit he paid to his deserted hometown:

> I went back to the town where I used to live, after thirty years, and I found it uninhabited. It's a town I knew with about seven or eight thousand inhabitants. It had one hundred and fifty when I returned... The people had left, just left. But someone had the idea of planting casuarinas along the streets of the town. I was there at night once, and it's a town where the wind blows a lot, it's at the foot of the Sierra Madre. And at night the casuarinas bellow and howl. And the wind. That's when I understood the loneliness of Comala, of that place.

Rulfo tells the story of Juan Preciado's reurn to Comala. Urged by his dying mother, he embarks on a quest to find his father. He finds a town populated by the ghosts of its former inhabitants, tortured souls wandering in a limbo, seeking absolution for their sins.

Pedro Páramo could be said to belong to a particular genre of literature – that of the speaking dead. The greatest exemplar of this genre is Edgar Lee Masters's *Spoon River Anthology*, wherein the deceased of the fictional small town of Spoon River deliver their own verse epitaphs. One is additionally reminded of the Mandelstam line 'yes, I am in the ground, but my lips are moving'. In Irish, Máirtín Ó Cadháin's *Cré na Cille* immediately springs to mind, and the manner in which his characters grumble about their graves is not unlike that of the dead in *Spoon River Anthology*. In Irish, the genre has further found expression in short-story writer Daithí Ó Muirí's extraordinary *Uaigheanna*, with its cast of night-watchmen, grave-diggers, suicides and lynch-mobs.

Pedro Páramo has twice been translated into English, most recently by Margaret Sayers Peden. Tomás Mac Siomóin has now translated it into Irish, and the results are astonishing. Mac Siomóin's consummate command of language makes his version in Irish seem like the most natural thing in the world. Lingering in Rulfo's novel there are multiple tropes from folk culture and oral narration, and these find a potent expression in Irish. Peden's English translation, in fact, often looks and sounds flat compared to the richness of Mac Siomóin's Irish. Thus 'that must mean she's still wandering like a lost soul' is 'ní foláir nó go bhfuil sí fós ar fán is ar fhaidreach'. Or 'then the sky took over the night' is rendered as 'ghlac an spéir seilbh ar an oíche'. Throughout Mac Siomóin's version there is a brilliant use of alliterative effects that demand to be read aloud. Again, compare and contrast the following:

> receding footsteps sounded to the jingle of spurs...

> cluineadh climirt na spor á bearnú ag fuaim na gcoiscéimeanna ag cúlú...

Like Mac Siomóin, Gabriel Rosenstock is one of Ireland's foremost literary intermediaries, establishing links between Irish language literature and the literatures of other countries, most notably those of the East. His latest venture is *Iqbal: dréachtaí próis is filíochta*, versions of poems and prose excerpts by Muslim poet and thinker Muhammad Iqbal (1877–1938). A prolific writer in Urdu, Arabic and Persian, Iqbal was also an ardent advocate of the revival of Islamic civilisation, and his vision of an independent state for Muslims in northwestern India inspired the eventual foundation of Pakistan, where he is revered as a national figure.

Through Rosenstock, Iqbal's poetry becomes Irish. Iqbal's haunting lament for the mosque at Cordoba could be seen to echo our own loss of a Gaelic order. But there is more than loss here, there are prescient warnings of the dangers of western individualism:

> D'fhéadfadh an fhéiniúlacht draíocht an domhain seo a scrios;
> Ach ní thuigeann gach éinne ár gcreideamh san Aon.

In his introduction, Michael Cronin speaks of the split in western thought between the individual and his environment, between the intellect and the senses ('scoilt in aigne an Iarthair idir an duine agus a thimpeallacht, idir an intinn agus na céadfaí'). Islam is not seen as puritanical, and we are reminded that Iqbal celebrated the senses, and particularly those of hearing and sight. His is a poetry which apprehends the world through the senses rather than philosophical constructs. Thus we have wonderful lines that apprehend the beauty of the physical world, replete with an exquisite lyric poise in Rosenstock's fluid versions:

> Tá carabhán na réaltaí an-chiúin
> Is gluaiseann gan clog a bhualadh

and

> Teachtaireacht an áthais shíoraí aige don ghairdín
> Tá sé tagtha chun péarlaí a fhuáil i seaicéad an róis

If it wasn't for Gabriel Rosenstock, who recently lent me *tríd an gcoill*, I'd probably never have heard of poet Séamas Cain and his strangely beautiful work. *tríd an gcoill* is what might be described as a poetic sonic field recording. It takes its inspiration from a walk through the woodland of Coill an Droma Mhóir in Co Clare in June 2008. Over the course of a hundred and twenty pages, the reader is immersed in a stream of words and word-clusters – 'lus, daol, loscán, éan, iasc' or 'lus, féileacán, frog, éan, éisc'. At one level it's a repetitive litany (I prefer the Irish word 'liodán'), but it's one full of surprises in its use of language, and particularly the genitive case in Irish. Thus one gets startling combinations such as 'féileacán blaoisce', 'lus blaoisce'. There is the fury of the wind ('fiúir na gaoithe'); the heavy scent of animals ('éan túise, éisc túise'); and there are images of animals scattering ('ruaigeadh préachán, ruaigeadh breac'). The overall effect is hypnotic, as if one is being led by a pied piper into the heart of the wood.

To actually quote from this book, or to give the reader a sense of how the text works, is no easy task. It is a work that needs not only to be read, but to be experienced, in its entirety. As much as it's based on sound patterns (whether random or deliberate, but more of that latter), *tríd an gcoill* is a visual work – to the left of every line is the image ^\\>//. Cain declares that he was 'concerned about its visuality, the selection of the font and the selection of the size of the font, the placement of images on the page'.

Cain's writing process uses randomisation – that is, he creates what he calls 'fields' of words, which are then fed into a computer and mathematically randomised. The result is what Cain calls a 'new juxtaposition'. But Cain also crafts this process, with nouns being carefully selected for their sound as well as for their sense. The computer-created patterns are then subject to intervention or editing. Cain very consciously restructures his text, and introduces themes of time (the last word in the poem is 'an clog') and limitation. He eschews nineteenth-century notions of the forest as 'wild' or 'other' or 'going on and on forever'. For Cain 'randomisation' is the very process in a real wood. Or as he puts it – 'on today's walk, we see a grey beetle on the big rock; but on yesterday's walk, this beetle was not there'.

Ultimately, though, I'm of the belief that 'to define is to destroy'; *tríd an gcoill* (available from **The.Red.Jasper@gmail.com**) does not need to be explained, it needs to be experienced. Just as David Bowie sang, 'Don't you wonder sometimes / 'Bout sound and vision', so does Cain re-jolt language to make us hear and see words as sound and as visual shapes, to sense their forms anew. And rather than being meaningless, Cain's radical word sculpture forces us to look at words in fresh contexts, and to ask ourselves what words actually mean.

Kit Fryatt

TUNES ARE OBLIGATORY

Leontia Flynn, *Drives* (Jonathan Cape, 2008), £9.
John Redmond, *MUDe* (Carcanet, 2008), £9.95.

I think I remember a time when rock journalists – thrifty sorts who would no more think of ditching a threadbare phrase than a duffel jacket in similar condition – spoke of the *difficult third album*. Now, with guitar-based pop music churning through its fifth or sixth renovation of the 1960s, and the limited resources of the genre more obvious than ever, we hear more about the difficulty of second albums. Success even of a modest sort removes songwriters from the sources that produced it in the first place, installs them in hotel bedrooms and on tour buses, only to desert them in a welter of songs about rain-lashed windscreens and the reliable indigestibility of the Best Western breakfast. Débuts can seem accomplished simply because they represent a decade or more's work; what follows must develop and extend the artists' range, yet appear quickly, before the public forgets them.

There's a poetic equivalent to this trajectory, though it includes fewer hours on the road and less dependence on rubbery croissants for subsistence. Poets are usually allowed to remain at home to nurse their ornery second-collection blues. However, Leontia Flynn, whose first book *These Days* (2004) probably induced more performance anxiety among young Irish poets than any published since the Beatles stopped gigging, has battled hers by staying on the move. *These Days*, though it includes poems of place and travel, rejects the affectations of worldliness. Its typical persona is a sheltered, nervy adolescent, not quite sure who Seamus Heaney is or which is an aubergine and which an avocado. Her contemporaries may have the glib veneer of gap-year cosmopolitanism; she, claiming self-effacingly that 'the furthest distances I've travelled / have been those between people. And what survives / of holidaying briefly in their lives', has the confidence to riff on 'An Arundel Tomb'. The pose of *These Days* is not one that can be sustained into maturity without coyness, and while Flynn has not attempted to strike it again in *Drives*, she has not found a fully convincing replacement for the engaging, fresh perspective of the first book.

The poet of *Drives* finds herself spending more time in the 'peculiar weather' of airports, and a number of the poems take the form of memoranda from European and American destinations. She is reliably disenchanted: finding 'too much *Rome* in Rome', and seeking out the 'worst tourist attraction, not just in Copenhagen, but maybe *anywhere*'. The double negative of 'New York', meanwhile, leaves us unsure whether its list of curiosities is delightful or dismaying. Flynn's gifts are intellectual and syntactic rather than verbally musical or imagistic: the poems give the impression of not quite knowing, at their beginning, where they're going to end up. The parallel with the poet's geographical dislocation is clear, but the reader might wonder whether the analogy is sufficient to render interesting a subject as commonplace as the disappointments of travel.

Interspersed among the postcards are poems about literary figures' medical complaints. Flynn writes powerfully about the body: one of the most extraordinary achievements in *These Days* is 'By My Skin', describing a childhood bedtime ritual whereby the speaker's father sings and dances as he treats his 'changeling child' with solid paraffin for a skin complaint. The poem plays the father's energy and motion against static but textured surroundings: patterned 1970s wallpaper, a candlewick bedspread, and of course, his daughter's inflamed skin. The poem seems to be animated by an unstated metaphor, the everyday one by which we describe aggravated surfaces in terms of noise and movement: 'loud', 'busy'. None of the pieces treating physical dysfunction in *Drives* is possessed of this power or subtlety. Flynn's unpretentious attitude, which puts no value on the recondite, has here led her to relay fairly familiar anecdotal material about writers and filmmakers: Samuel Beckett's many psychosomatic illnesses, Alfred Hitchcock's phobias, Elizabeth Bishop's alcoholism and respiratory problems, Robert Lowell's heart attack. Lacking the interest of gossipy novelty or verbal density, these poems suffer from an *ennui* oddly similar to the disillusioned-tourist series. The unevenness of *Drives* suggests that Flynn's success is as disconcerting to her as to her less dexterous contemporaries, and that her apparently intuitive aesthetic is no longer serving her as well as it might. Nonetheless, the very best poem in the collection, 'Our Fathers', is of this clue-following sort, suggesting in its interrupted open-endedness a direction for Flynn's (no doubt uneasy, if not difficult) third collection.

Both Flynn and her slightly older contemporary John Redmond share (with many of their peers) an indifference to identity politics and an unselfconscious attitude to Irish culture, neither ignoring it nor assuming it exceptional. Their postmodern savvy was facilitated by poets of the preceding generation like Paul Muldoon and Paul Durcan, both of whom, however, make intractable precursors. There is not much mileage left in wisecracking sub-Muldoonery, and indeed Muldoon sometimes seems intent on running that particular jalopy into the scrapyard himself. Durcan's copious poetic does not permit of development by any but the foolhardy, and foolhardiness is not the fault of Ireland's younger poets. A new ease is evident among them, but anxiety of influence remains, and we might also see that in the 'disappearance of Ireland' (the phrase is Justin Quinn's, responding critically to the poetic moment of which he is himself a part) a resource has been lost.

John Redmond's first collection, *Thumb's Width* (2001) is less of a farewell to Ireland, or to nationalism, than to Irish exceptionalism. In 'Sloane', for example, a glimpse of a 'gorgeous' member of that urban tribe prompts the barfly speaker to free-associate, the proliferating puns forming an analogy with his growing randiness:

> And yet if *so long*
> is really *as close to slán*
> (and this is my father's old slogan)
> *as Sri Lanka*
> *to Ceylon*
>
> how far can it be from *sláinte* to *slán*?

More interesting than the derivative manner of this poem are its atmospherics. It is an *aisling* of a kind – *mise Sasana* – in which Redmond has captured a distinctly post-imperial mood. A belief in the pristine animates both the 'old slogan' drawing attention to one of a tiny number of Irish loanwords in English and the implicit post-colonial parallel '*as Sri Lanka / to Ceylon*' – but the poet, though not ignorant of political resonance, is lasciviously immersed in verbal textures. The Sloane, meanwhile, *is* ignorant, or at least unaware, of the speaker's half-cringing, half-contemptuous regard. No doubt if she were asked (she is not, perhaps significantly) she would say history is to blame.

MUDe is at once more ambitious and more limited than *Thumb's Width*. The relatively traditional and domestic subject matter of the first collection permitted excursions into history and politics (as well as a very informative disquisition on Dexy's Midnight Runners, who produced perhaps the definitive difficult third album of the 1980s). *MUDe*'s preoccupation with subcultures draws it towards the apolitical and interpersonal, in spite of its hefty cultural studies epigraphs. The first part of the book is largely concerned with the *mores* of the automobile, especially those of the mid-western United States (Redmond worked at the University of Minnesota between 2001 and 2003), though three poems at the end of this first section continue the more familiar and familial themes of *Thumb's Width*. Redmond has a gift for pastiche, and the liveliest of the short poems in *MUDe*, 'The Clown Lounge' and 'Grand Theft America', are ventriloqual and impressionistic, presenting a variety of American voices without authorial comment. A coincidence serves to illustrate in little the difference between his approach and Flynn's – both poets end a poem with a version of the catchphrase associated with the NPR motoring programme *Car Talk*: 'don't drive like my brother!' Flynn embeds her reference in a further allusion to *Annie Hall*, which is in turn part of an open letter to Karen Blixen, turning the cheery sign-off into a Gothic threat; Redmond is content to register it as part of the soundscape of Minnesotan life.

That attention to aural texture is crucial to *MUDe*'s eponymous second section, a long poem which reads like the transcription of an online role-playing game, or Multi User Dimension. Redmond chooses a nearly obsolescent form of MUD, a text-based Dungeons and Dragons game. Those readers who have twenty-five-year-old memories of playing such games alone and remain unaware of their continuing (if self-consciously retro) internet currency will be delighted by Redmond's affectionate mimicry of their eccentric narrative style. The idiom is exclamatory yet chillingly flat, straining to evoke a scene with unusual adjectives and verbs which succeed only in drawing attention to themselves, attentive for the purposes of gameplay to inanimate objects which as a side effect achieve a curious galvanic life:

> Your ten-year-old self is here
> A little ball is here
>
> [...]
>
> Your ten-year-old self spreads his arms wide in the manner of a
> goalkeeper.
> He is guarding the fireplace for all he is worth!
>
> You hear the wind slumping up and down the chimney.

Redmond brings the same talent for imitation to the chatroom commentary of his imaginary players. His cast of nerds is plausible and predictable, though rather understated – readers with even minimal experience of internet fora will have uncovered more grotesque specimens in their virtual lives. The narrative sections of 'MUDe' are interesting because they engage, from a more radical perspective, with the questions of authenticity broached in *Thumb's Width*. MUD-narrative shares with poetry a self-consciousness, a concern to enact and evoke, a level of linguistic estrangement. But it is poetry disassembled, without the illusion of inevitable form. Redmond makes bafflingly little of the forms provided by gameplay convention: for example, rather than trying to incorporate the 'reset' of the MUD into the poem's fabric, he uses it merely to effect a fade-out. His weaving of a sub-Tolkien fantasy with a situation almost equally clichéd – the rural Irish family riven by unspoken conflict – has the potential to be touching, and though most of the lyrics in 'MUDe' are parodic, some of them make a pleasingly crunchy noise:

> with a swish
>   of slow hooked crashes
>
> the crispest
> of crisp blades insist
>
> on their rich persistent struggle
>
>   this
>   rough indoor drizzle

MUDe is the work of a poet who has not explored his limits, one who is working within his competency: it is not experimental enough. Like many difficult albums, it substitutes the inessential for the vital, and though interesting seems ultimately ephemeral. Poetry and pop music are not very different in this regard at least: concepts are optional; *tunes* are obligatory.

Val Nolan

WHERE DO WE GO FROM HERE?

Patrick Moran, *Green* (Salmon Poetry, 2008), €12.
Mark Granier, *The Sky Road* (Salmon Poetry, 2007), €12.
Jean O'Brien, *Lovely Legs* (Salmon Poetry, 2009), €12.
Enda Wyley, *To Wake to This* (Dedalus Press, 2009), €12.

Four new titles – three from Salmon and one from Dedalus – offer a shifting lens on the responses of contemporary poetry in the Republic to recent changes in Irish society. While the work of Patrick Moran, Mark Granier, Jean O'Brien, and Enda Wyley lacks any overt political or social commentary, there is a prevailing uncertainty in all their collections – from O'Brien's house-moving sequence to Granier's wanderlust – which betrays these introverted lyrics as poems of their time. A piece like Moran's 'London Irish', which until lately might have been considered old-fashioned, takes on a new relevance in the current climate, while O'Brien's pointedly titled 'Before', or her silage bales 'tightly / wrapped in funeral black', signal the end of an idealised, arguably non-existent rural Irish arcadia. Wyley, meanwhile, retreats from all such notions into the realm of maternal bliss, while Granier mostly abandons such fancy for the highways of the world at large. It is notable too that poetry about deceased parents is a presence in all four collections (though somewhat less in Wyley, who covered this topic extensively in 1998's *Socrates in the Garden*), as if to suggest a lack of direction in contemporary writing arising from Irish poetry's parental figures being largely deceased (and so unsatisfying to reproach), or Northern (culturally and commercially estranged), or simply enjoying the hard-won exile of American or British universities.

Of the four, it is Tipperary's Patrick Moran who most diligently grounds himself in the familiar. *Green*, his second collection, opens with a statement of intent where the poet challenges himself to accomplish things the hard way. He wonders if he 'should have lived / like all the others who just set a time-clock / or flick a switch to summon heat'; and, while the query and response structure of the poem leads to a somewhat predictable result ('if I'd done that, what would I have known / about fire's glow and afterglow'), it does demonstrate that, for Moran, process is part and parcel of result.

Yet the poet never allows blind dedication to tradition to limit his gaze, and the strongest poems in *Green* document the collision of the past and present – that interface we consciously ignore, 'where rumbling earthmovers / transform the little fields'. Here Moran finds – if not exactly something new – a suitable subject for his nuanced eye. More often than not this takes the form of 'antipathy between my art and life,' the struggle between the worlds of erudition and popular culture, neither of which exists satisfactorily on its own. A night spent 'absorbing Nietzsche's *Weltanschauung*' leads to nothing but 'pent-up, tongue-tied lust', while on the other hand Jimi Hendrix's talent and charisma culminates in 'a drugs overdose / in some girl's rented flat'. The arrangement of the collection itself further emphasises the stupidity of sundering the intellectual from the entertaining, and the Hendrix poem, linguistically staid as though its subject strayed too far from Moran's 'potholed boreen', is directly preceded by 'Words for Philip Larkin', a much more successful admonishment of the single-interest individual:

> Behold me now: bald, heavy-jowled;
> wearing thick glasses, hearing aids.
> My monkish personality
> has failed the elemental world:
> I have no stake, no wife, no kids.
> At this stage, what is left for me?

'Botched imaginings,' perhaps, but little else. It is a harsh lyric, which some scribblers may find too close to the bone, but certainly it is honest. So too are the poet's efforts at rebuking Yeats's mortifying narcissism: 'Imagine fretting that a play you wrote / send out some men the English shot?' he asks from a twenty-first century Ireland which, to borrow a phrase, has changed utterly. Only with embarrassment can he admit his own desire to sway the hearts of 'knowing countrymen' and cause them to 'spare one hedgerow from their blades', a revelation which deliciously complicates an otherwise straightforward squib.

'At Inniskeen', a piece in memory of Patrick Kavanagh, is even more intriguing: 'Where are they now, the ripening girls / you coveted at dances?' Where, Moran wonders, are the priests, the old women, and the legendary footballers? All of them are gone and yet Kavanagh remains, a whole community 'risen from your pen'. 'At Inniskeen' is a nostalgic poem to be sure, but, as with many of the pieces here, Moran's elegiac blend of loss and wonder is motivated more by how Ireland has been portrayed by writers in the past than by the passing of these departed wordsmiths' lifestyles.

Throughout *Green*, the poet eulogises not just the 'blazing sods' and 'grazing for hay' of rural Ireland; he bemoans the overwriting of that milieu. It is telling, so, that many of the poems here revolve around the rituals of death. Moran does not know what's next for small-town

Ireland, but that confusion is his greatest resource; it forces him to scrutinise the end of everything he knows and he responds, often beautifully though simply, with a poetry of curates, candles and contrition. Eluded by the future, or at least by the language necessary to articulate it, Moran moves metaphorically into the 'century-old mansion' of the parish priest's house and takes it on himself to grimly officiate at the interment of an older Ireland. 'Were these the pieties we clutched?' he asks, 'So absolute. So long ago.' Poems such as 'Wake', 'Removal of Remains', and 'November' all explore the 'gatherings and scatterings' of Irish funerary customs, but it is the Cathleen Ní Houlihan figure of 'Her Dying' – notwithstanding its clear familial origins – which best enunciates the decline of rural communities and the uselessness of old allegories in the modern age:

> Her finger-joints had gone arthritic, gnarled.
> Dribbling there, staring into vacancy,
> she wilted under a regimen of pills
> that barely eased her pain, her disarray.

The Sky Road, by Mark Granier, is the exact opposite: a much looser, more varied collection which at times is bound together only by its willingness to go anywhere. *The Sky Road* is a book about journeys; where Moran's poetry was localised and communal, Granier's strolls through Swords, drives through the Sally Gap, swims off the coast of Vancouver by night and tumbles from the deck of San Francisco's Golden Gate. A former winner of the Vincent Buckley Prize, Granier has produced a book 'nudged, absently, by the planet' itself, a collection in which Irish landscapes blend into those from around the world. 'Singapore – London – Dublin' is the title of one piece; 'Here, There' the title of another. The poet's conception of contemporary Irish identity is lyrical and globalised. The streets and boulevards of foreign capitals run seamlessly into Mount Street Bridge or the dual carriageway at Kilmacanogue, and, though the occasional flippancy of some poems here distracts, *The Sky Road* negotiates the slipstream between the Irish and the international in a suitably satisfying fashion.

Furthermore, and refreshingly unlike many contemporary Irish poets, Granier is unafraid to extend the international influence backwards, to a childhood defined not by Fáilte Ireland hokum but by imports such as *The Man from U.N.C.L.E.* and *Doctor Who*. This, of course, is not to say there aren't hints of a more insular past in *The Sky Road*. 'Our dark / island kept itself to itself,' he says at one point, but overall his willingness to acknowledge the patchwork of influences on his generation makes his recollections more sincere. Yes, the ghosts of old Ireland still wander

Granier's byways, but they share the airwaves with garbled broadcasts from the BBC and with the contrails of aircraft bound for everywhere. Moreover, and unlike Moran's *Green*, the spirits here will not easily be put to rest. They remain part of the conversation, communing with both the landscape and the poet: 'Are you dead?' Granier asks of a familiar, only to receive the ambiguous answer: 'I'm still here'.

On the N6, the N1, and the N11 – all major routes emanating from Dublin to urban centres around the island – Granier encounters both shades of the past and the 'curse or gift' of the present's unfulfilled aspirations. One particularly subtle stanza conflates these concerns with the passing innocence of childhood:

> Thin, tall, armless, a thawing ghost
> of a snowman – a milestone
> for where miles go.

Elsewhere he reads the country's new roads like lines on the hand of the nation, following them as they take the load of a national consciousness preoccupied with notions of modernity and vacuous success. For the most part, these are poems 'delicately arranging their way', and, arriving at the many destinations of *The Sky Road*, Granier makes the admirable point that 'One's uneventful flight / is another's tenfold-night'.

Lovely Legs by Jean O'Brien is a different kind of book again, one in which the faraway promises of jet-trails are constrained by the domesticity of skylight frames. A lively, readable collection concerned with the intricacies of relationships and the many moral contradictions of society, *Lovely Legs* follows the arcs of 'lives on a fulcrum', honing in repeatedly on moments of change and realisation. Bee poems such as 'Masks', which opens the collection, make clear that the book's presiding deity is Plath, though O'Brien successfully resists the kind of easy mimicry which might have compromised her own perspective. Poems here discuss femininity and children, but they are all very clearly in O'Brien's voice, a seemingly carefree lilt which nonetheless exudes complexity and depth. Old stories of 'hope and romance' dissolve into poems that actively resist (and sometimes ridicule) the past, while other pieces here lean heavily on popular culture such as *The Simpsons* or the word soup of 'magnetic poetry' which clings to refrigerator doors across the country.

Nature too is everywhere in *Lovely Legs*, but, in contrast to the 'weedy gravel, neglected lawns' of Moran's *Green* or Granier's 'Suburban Woods', it is the cultivated nature of yards and gardens which predominates. Similarly, the many poems here addressed to or about O'Brien's 'younger self' attempt to civilise the unruliness of childhood, and, in a self-mythologising turn, lessons are always learnt. Often they are comically disproportionate to the experience, such as when O'Brien recalls how, as children travelling along redbrick lanes, she and her friends were approached by a pervert, a Joycean encounter which 'made us remember / to hurry home for tea.'

Further poems explore notions of poetry and language themselves, images which 'escape us' or verses which don't have 'enough words to go around'. Frequently O'Brien's writing focuses on people's inability to communicate, such as the last speaker of the Uru tongue who 'has kept herself to herself / since the second-last person / who spoke Uru died.' Meanwhile,

> Truth is a labyrinth, obscured
> like the alburnum that lies between
> the sapwood and the heartwood
> we sense it just below the surface.

It is only in the lyric, in the poetic rush, that true connections can actually occur. Poetry is an interactive art, one where 'coded messages are posted / in limited language', and unpacking the layers of meaning in these communiqués is part of the pleasure of this dense book. O'Brien's verse – like her bees – is 'buzzing and busy'. Her world of 'flat, broad horizons' is one seen 'with compound eyes', and her warm response to Paula Meehan's poetry is equally applicable to her own; amid all the 'noise of traffic', the 'clang of tram bells', there is also 'the brightening hum of her words' which, 'like a modern day Angelus / calls us home'.

Where O'Brien's collection includes a number of poems about her parents and their passing, Enda Wyley's *To Wake to This* is, in contrast, dominated by snapshots of children, from their 'blip-blipping' in the womb to their learning to read with a 'huge book / a block of pale corn-light' wedged between their fingers. Wyley, who also writes fiction for younger readers, adeptly conveys the bond between mother and infant, with the majority of *To Wake to This* speaking hopefully to the poet's aspirations for the future, certainly more so than either Moran's *fin-de-siècle* aesthetic or the 'Abandoned Monastery' of Granier's Ireland. 'Little heart / not yet hurt, / beat on', she says in the opening poem, a tender sketch of innocence recovered through the joys of parenthood, but the simplicity of this poem is deceptive; an unpretentious bedtime ditty, it yet sets the scene for the collection's sustained interrogation of contemporary poetry's obsession with the past. Surely, Wyley seems to be saying, the future is what writers ought to be looking towards?

'If we had known / we would not / have slept so long' begins the title poem, and awakenings – to future possibilities as much as to gorgeous mornings and to night-time feeds – recur again and again in a largely discursive collection. Wyley attacks her themes relentlessly, from a multitude of angles, and though the poems are debating constantly with one another, the result is just the right side of a mêlée. But then that is part of the style Wyley has adopted in *To Wake to This*: a steady internal tension predicated on the friction she divines between the past and the future. Offsetting memory against the uncanny art and statuary of modern public spaces, a pair of poems translate 'echoes of what we were' into an imagery of what we've yet to become. Elsewhere, 'Caitlín Maude Sings on the Radio' and allows dreams of the future to intersect with a recording of that 'black-haired bard long dead, / still clear-pitched, rhythmical, true.' However it is the poem 'Gold Wallpaper' which best typifies Wyley's conception of a day-to-day existence which extends beyond the merely linear. A progression backwards is always part of moving forward here, and, in this poem, the future of a relationship is ensured by a night spent 'finding old houses' and stripping back their wallpaper:

> Until in one crumbling mansion,
> your fingers touched mine and from the thick walls
> fat with damp we stripped back seventies swirls,
> sixties floral patterns, the formal fifties lines –
> and found gold.

Likewise, 'Gold Wallpaper' is of a piece with the focus on 'strange things in strange places' found elsewhere in the book. Wyley, mercifully, has little interest in an ordinary life made more ordinary again, and her poetry is always looking for the striking or unusual, such as the lucky man startled 'by the tenor / singing in soprano / the poem of another man / writing as a woman / in the seventeenth century'.

Writing for 'the page within', Wyley's poems declare that – like it or not – we live in the future now, an idea or a flawed ideal we have constructed from pieces of the past. Moran, Granier and O'Brien wrestle with this realisation in their own way, but it is Wyley who puts it best when she writes, in 'Notebook Shop':

> There is no end to where our poems go –
> anywhere to be free, not to be trapped
> in these fine and beautiful books
> that are hungry for a scribble,
> a dream, the rush of a word.

Justin Quinn

THE LONG WAIT

Paul Valéry, translated by Peter Dale, *Charms and Other Pieces* (Anvil Press Poetry, 2007), £11.95.

The received wisdom about poetry in translation is that it doesn't exist; that it is impossible to convey both the meaning and beauty of a poem across the border between two languages. But the opposite is in fact the case: sometimes there is no poetry without translation. A large number of major poets found themselves in translation, and more generally, the entire English tradition was shaped through its contact with Latin, French, Irish and Scottish poetry, among others. The contact with the idiom, imagery and rhythm of poetry in a foreign language enables and expands the poetic imagination. This is as true of Housman as it is of Eliot.

A further aspect of poetry and translation is timing. For instance, in retrospect, it is easy to say that Italian sonnets came to Anglophone poetry at the right moment. Arguably, Peter Dale's translation of Valéry's *Charmes* comes at exactly the wrong time. Valéry's heyday in English was in the first half of the twentieth century, when writers such as Wallace Stevens, F R Leavis, T S Eliot and Allen Tate welcomed him to their language. Now his combination of abstraction, exclamation and etiolated meditation seems out of step with things. In contrast with previous times, one rarely turns to poetry for philosophical argument, and large-scale intellectual preoccupations within poems are considered a weakness. Abstraction itself is thought to be negative, as though to move away from immediate reality and demotic idiom could only enervate poetry. This tendency is particularly strong in Ireland and Britain – one cannot imagine a poet being praised there for his or her abstractions. It must be admitted that, yes, abstraction can enervate poetry, but, used correctly, it can also energise it, furnishing it with new horizons, emotions and radical repatternings of experience. The memory of a landscape viewed from a plane changes your perception when you spend a day walking through it.

Thus, we might say that Valéry returns at exactly the right time, to display lost possibilities to English poetry, the same that once animated Sidney, Milton, Blake and Yeats – all poets who engaged passionately in philosophical abstraction, and yet who never confused the writing of tracts with the writing of poetry. An excellent example of this is Valéry's 'La Pythie', which refers to the Greek oracle, Pythia, and is about the connections between time, language and subjectivity. What is it like to be such an oracle, to have large forces speak through you, to see suddenly the vistas of human history – past, passing and to come – and express them in words? It is something quite terrible, as the first few verses make clear, with their violent, physical description of the woman:

> La Pythie exhalant la flamme
> De naseaux durcis par l'encens,
> Haletante, ivre, hurle!
>
> [...]
>
> – Ah! maudite!... Quels maux je souffre!
> Toute ma nature est un gouffre!
> Hélas! Entr'ouverte aux esprits,
> J'ai perdu mon propre mystère!

Her physical and mental suffering is profound. She has lost herself: when she looks within, all she encounters is a huge gulf. But her prophecies are impossible without this gulf, because this is the space of visions:

> Alors, par cette vagabonde
> Morte, errante, et lune à jamais,
> Soit l'eau des mers surprise, et l'onde
> Astreinte à d'éternels sommets!
> Que soient les humains faits statues,
> Les cœurs figés, les âmes tues,
> Et par les glaces de mon œil,
> Puisse un peuple de leurs paroles
> Durcir en un peuple d'idoles
> Muet de sottise et d'orgueil!

Here whole aeons of history are surveyed, and the impression is of terrific velocity and clairvoyance; there is also a large geographical extent, as though seas and summits were contained within the body of the woman. This velocity and these vistas are the mainstay of the poem, and indeed of Valéry's poetry in general. To write a poetry which encompassed them, Valéry avoided the personal, the romantic, the Wordsworthian anecdote. 'La Pythie' eventually comes to an idea of language that speaks through not only the Pythia, but all people. Language is not something we master, but something that masters us and makes us. But just as Keats's 'Ode on a Grecian Urn' does not become part of the tradition purely thanks to its concluding metaphysical equation, neither does Valéry's poem impress us only because of the epigram of the last stanza. Rather it is because he has taken us on such an intense journey to reach his conclusion, as we remember 'les humains faits statues, / Les cœurs figés, les âmes tues', all viewed through the Pythia's eye. The poem is so far from lived experience that its gaze is almost commensurate with a god's. This is its divine abstraction.

Poetry, like some other discourses, helps us understand the times we live in, on the local level, as say, in Yeats's 'Easter 1916', or the civilisational level as in Tennyson's 'In Memoriam'. It is difficult to pinion Valéry to particular historical circumstances, whereas Yeats and Tennyson invite us to do exactly that. The disasters and difficulties that Valéry witnessed in his lifetime become generalised, and he uses the patterns and figures of Greek mythology to meditate upon them, though he does not ask us to believe in Parcas and Pythias. It is yet another 'mythical method', different from Joyce's, but no less available to its time, and perhaps more available to our times than Joyce's work now is. After all, Yeats's poem can never be of central interest to general readers beyond Ireland, just as Tennyson's cannot be to readers without a professional or emotional investment in nineteenth-century England. Valéry, I would argue, by virtue of his abstraction, still remains available.

Throughout I have refrained from quoting Dale's translations. When Alistair Elliot translated *La Jeune Parque* in 1997, he chose not to replicate the rhyme structure of the original, opting instead for blank verse over the rhymed alexandrines of the French; when Derek Mahon translated 'Le Cimetière Marin', he rhymed it but did not conform to the pattern of the original; when James Merrill translated 'Palme' he maintained the rhyme scheme. Merrill's and Mahon's are the finest renditions in English, but it must be noted that neither translated as much as Elliot or Dale. The latter has chosen to maintain the rhyme scheme and that choice, if not the results, is admirable. Dale lacks the craft to carry off the job, and on almost every page there are gaffes of idiom and idea. On occasion, grammar is sacrificed for rhyme (verse eleven of 'La Pythie'). Often, where Valéry's lines are simple and clear, Dale's are contorted to get the rhyme. A few examples:

> Et mon triangle d'émeraude
> Tire sa langue à double fil…
> Bête je suis, mais bête aiguë,
> De qui le venin quoique vil
> Laisse loin la sage ciguë!
>
> My emerald triangle advances
> Its darting tongue of double thread…
> A dumb beast, me, but fly I am;

Though vile, my venom, given its head,
Leaves far behind nice hemlock's dram!

–'ÉBAUCHE D'UN SERPENT'

Quand le ciel couleur d'une joue
Laisse enfin les yeux le chérir...

When sky the colour of a cheek
Allows the sight a cherished eyeing...

– 'LA CEINTURE'

Les mains pleines de seins vivants,
Entre mes bras aux belles anses
Mon abîme a bu les immenses
Profondeurs qu'apportent les vents!

With living breasts my hands full,
Within my arms, lovely and round,
My void has tasted the profound
Heights carried on the wind's pull!

–'LA PYTHIE'

The awkardness in the first two examples is clear enough. In the third, the 'wind's pull' is unidiomatic, and present only for the rhyme. But when one looks back at the line that necessitates 'pull', we see that the word order is inverted. Moreover, 'pull' is bad because it ends with the idea of a single object, whereas the original has a plural, and because it is the word 'winds', it throws open, rather than closes, the horizon. The only line translated well is the third here, but even then we have the egregious insertion of 'heights' immediately after, which makes unidirectional what has multiple, wandering movements in the original.

It is a thankless job to translate Valéry. It is as though the French language will not release him in English in extended passages (though it might in Italian or Spanish, tongues of Valéry's beloved Mediterranean). Merrill and Mahon show that an English Valéry is both possible and desirable. But the wait continues.

Notes on Contributors

Michelle Cahill is a Sydney-based poet. Her first collection, *The Accidental Cage* (Interactive Press, 2006), was shortlisted for the 2007 Judith Wright Prize. Her poems have appeared in *Meanjin, Southerly, Asia Literary Review*, and are forthcoming in *Drunken Boat* and *Antipodes*.

Liam Carson is the director of the IMRAM Irish Language Literature Festival, and a publicist with publishing house Cois Life. His reviews, articles and essays have appeared in *Fortnight, The Irish Review, New Hibernia Review, Comhar* and the *Irish Examiner*.

Jennifer Compton lives on the outskirts of Melbourne. She is a poet and playwright who also writes prose. Her short story 'Not His Real Name' was published in *The Best New Zealand Fiction*, while her stage play *The Big Picture* was performed in Sydney and Perth. Her poetry has most recently appeared in *Poetry New Zealand, The Rialto* and *Poetry London*.

Helen Cooney is a member of the School of English, Trinity College Dublin. She teaches and researches in the fields of medieval and Renaissance English and Scottish literature, and describes herself as an 'aspiring' poet.

Heather Craig is a poet and critic. Her work has appeared in various Canadian poetry journals, including *Room* and *The Antigonish Review*. She was recently awarded both an Arts New Brunswick Creation Grant to complete her first poetry collection, and a second prize from the Atlantic Writing Competition for the unpublished manuscript.

Michael Cronin teaches in Dublin City University. *Transforming Ireland: Challenges, Critiques, Resources*, co-edited with Peadar Kirby and Debbie Ging, will be published by Manchester University Press in 2009.

Peter Denman is Dean of the Faculty of Arts at NUI, Maynooth. His publication credits include *Samuel Ferguson: The Literary Achievement* (as author), *Poetry Ireland Review* 34–37 (as editor), and *Seán Ó Tuama – Death in the Land of Youth: Collected Poems* (as translator).

Ryan Dennis grew up on a dairy farm in Western New York State. He attended Alfred State College, The University of Iowa, and NUI, Galway.

Tom Duddy lives and works in Galway. He has had poems published in Irish and UK magazines, including *Envoi, Magma, Smiths Knoll, Southword, The Dark Horse, THE SHOp, Seam*, and *The Rialto*. A chapbook, *The Small Hours*, was published in 2006 by HappenStance Press.

Katherine Duffy lives in Dublin, where she works as a translator in the Houses of the Oireachtas. Dedalus Press published her first collection, *The Erratic Behaviour of Tides*, in 1999. Her second, *Swallow the Black*, is forthcoming in 2010, also from Dedalus Press.

Tom French's first collection, *Touching the Bones* (Gallery Press, 2001), was awarded the Forward Prize for Best First Collection in 2002. His second collection is titled *The Fire Step* (Gallery Press, 2009). Recent poems have appeared or are due to appear in *THE SHOp* and *The Manchester Review*.

Kit Fryatt is a lecturer in English at the Mater Dei Institute of Education, Dublin. She is involved in running Mater Dei's Irish Centre for Poetry Studies, and co-edits its web journal, *POST*. She is co-organiser of 'Wurm im Apfel', a poetry reading series held in Dublin.

Desmond Graham is Professor of Poetry Emeritus at Newcastle University. A collection of poetry, *The Green Parakeet*, will be published this year by Flambard Press.

Eamon Grennan's most recent poetry collections are *Out of Breath* (Gallery Press, 2007) and *Matter of Fact* (Graywolf Press, 2008). A collection of his critical essays, *Facing the Music: Irish Poetry in the Twentieth Century* was published by Creighton University Press in 1999. He taught for many years in the English Department of Vassar College, and now teaches in the graduate writing programs of Columbia and NYU.

Seamus Heaney's début collection, *Death of a Naturalist*, was published by Faber and Faber in 1966. His most recent poetry collection is *District and Circle* (Faber and Faber, 2006). He was awarded the Nobel Prize for Literature in 1995.

Tom Hubbard's latest book is the novel *Marie B.* (Ravenscraig Press, 2009), about the painter and diarist Marie Bashkirtseff. A 'wandering Scot', he has worked in France, the US, Hungary and Ireland.

Cate Huguelet was born in Chicago, and has completed an MA in writing at NUI, Galway. She has been a featured reader in Galway's 'Over the Edge' poetry series, and was awarded second place in the 2007 'Over the Edge New Writer of the Year' competition. Her work has been featured in *The Stinging Fly*.

Edward Jarvis has been published in *The American Voice*, *Red Rock Review*, and elsewhere. His first collection of poetry, *Palimpsest*, was published in 2001 by Sullen Arts Press.

Gerard Lee is a graduate of the M Phil in Creative Writing in Trinity College, Dublin. He has published poetry in *Poetry Ireland Review*, *THE SHOp*, *Southword* and *An Sionnach*. He was selected as part of the Poetry Ireland Introduction Series in 2007.

James J McAuley's first poetry collection was published by Dolmen Press in 1965. He spent over thirty years teaching poetry as co-director in the Creative Writing Programme at Eastern Washington University. His *New & Selected Poems* was published by Dedalus Press in 2005.

Iggy McGovern's first collection *The King of Suburbia* (Dedalus Press, 2005) received the inaugural Glen Dimplex New Writers Award for Poetry.

Val Nolan teaches creative writing and contemporary literature at NUI, Galway.

D Nurkse is the author of nine books of poetry, most recently *The Border Kingdom* (Alfred Knopf, 2008).

Sean O'Brien is Professor of Creative Writing at Newcastle University. His most recent collection of poems, *The Drowned Book*, was awarded both the Forward and the T S Eliot Prize in 2007. His first novel, *Afterlife*, will be published by Picador in August.

Mary O'Donnell's first three collections *Reading the Sunflowers in September* (1990), *Spiderwoman's Third Avenue Rhapsody* (1993) and *Unlegendary Heroes* (1998), were published by Salmon Poetry. A sixth collection, *The Ark Builders*, will appear from Arc Publications (UK) later in 2009. She is a member of Aosdána.

Edward O'Dwyer is from Limerick and was educated at UL and UCC. He is previously published in *The Stony Thursday Book*, *Southword*, *The SHOp*, *Agenda*, *Revival*, *Crannóg*, *The Journal*, *Tinteán*, *Five Words*, and *Census: The Seven Towers Anthology*. He also featured with two other poets in the chapbook *Revival: Trio*, published by Revival Press in 2007.

Tony O'Dwyer has had work published in *Poetry Ireland Review*, the *Cúirt Annual*, *Crannóg* and elsewhere. A runner up in the Patrick Kavanagh Award in 1999, his first collection *Off Guard* was published by Bradshaw Books in 2003. Editor of *Crannóg Magazine* (**crannogmagazine.com**), he co-runs the publishing house WordsontheStreet (**wordsonthestreet.com**).

Barra Ó Seaghdha writes about poetry, history, cultural politics and music (or combinations thereof) in such publications as the *Dublin Review of Books* (**drb.ie**) and the *Journal of Music in Ireland*.

Paul Perry's third collection, *The Last Falcon and Small Ordinance*, will be published in 2010 by Dedalus Press. He is working with Ruta Suchodolskyte on *108 Moons*, a book of translations of the Lithuanian poet Jurga Ivanauskaitė.

Justin Quinn's translations of Petr Borkovec, *From the Interior: Poems 1995–2005*, were published last year by Seren.

Peter Richardson is a retired airline worker living in Gatineau, Quebec. His latest book is *Sympathy for the Couriers*, published in 2007 by Véhicule Press, Montreal.

Padraig Rooney's *In The Bonsai Garden* (Raven Arts Press) won the Patrick Kavanagh Award for poetry in 1986. His second collection, *The Escape Artist* (Smith/Doorstop Books, 2006), won The Poetry Business Book and Pamphlet Competition in 2006. He has received two bursaries from the Irish Arts Council/An Chomhairle Ealaíon, and is the 2009 winner of the Strokestown International Poetry Prize. He lives in Basel, Switzerland.

Ana María Sánchez-Arce was born in Sant Joan de Vilatorrada, near Barcelona, and has lived in England since 1997. She is a Lecturer in English Literature at Sheffield Hallam University.

David Sergeant currently lectures in English at Oxford. His publication credits include *PN Review, Stand, The London Magazine, Envoi* and *Acumen*.

Timothy Shea received an MFA from Southern Illinois University, Carbondale, USA. His poetry has appeared or is forthcoming in *Poetry London, Poet Lore, RATTLE* and *New Madrid*. He lives in Herrin, Illinois.

Peter Sirr was born in Waterford. A winner of the Patrick Kavanagh Award, he is a former director of the Irish Writers' Centre and a former editor of *Poetry Ireland Review*. His poetry collections, all published by Gallery Press, include *The Ledger of Fruitful Exchange* (1995) and *Selected Poems* (2004). He is a member of Aosdána.

Dawn Wood was born in Omagh. Her first collection of poems is *Quarry* (Templar Poetry, 2008). Recently she has had poems published in *Poetry Review, PN Review, Edinburgh Review, Poetry London* and *TLS*.

Howard Wright lectures in the History of Fine and Applied arts at the University of Ulster, Belfast. Recent poems have appeared in *The North, Cyphers* and *The Frogmore Papers*. His first full collection, *King of Country*, is forthcoming from Blackstaff Press.

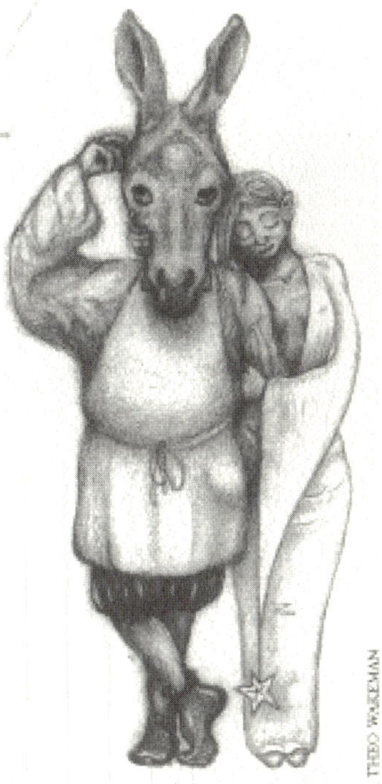
THEO WAKEMAN